How MYTHS
ABOUT LANGUAGE
AFFECT EDUCATION

What Every Teacher Should Know

David Johnson
Kennesaw State University

Ann Arbor
THE UNIVERSITY OF MICHIGAN PRESS

Dedication

This book is dedicated to the memory of my mother, Tommie Johnson, who was my first English teacher.

I would also like to dedicate this book to those who continue to teach me about language: my father, Gene Johnson; my wife, Priya; my daughters, Emily and Sarah; my in-laws, KM and Ann Mathew; and most especially the many ESL students I have taught through the years.

Acknowledgments

I would like to acknowledge the many colleagues who have contributed to this project. First, I owe a debt of gratitude to Judy Holzman (Kennesaw State University) for allowing me to participate in her U.S. Department of Education grant. With the support of this grant, I was able to have the time needed to finish this project. She is a dedicated colleague and admirable person.

I also wish to thank the many colleagues who have read earlier versions of this book and provided valuable comments. I especially wish to thank Margie Berns (Purdue University) and David Schmidt (Kennesaw State University). I also would like to thank my wife, Priya Johnson, for reading multiple drafts of this book and for marking all my typos. I want to thank Paul and Aya Matsuda (Arizona State University) for helping me with the example of Japanese postpositions.

I owe a special thank you to Kelly Sippell at the University of Michigan Press for all of her help during the entire process. The book is far better because of her insights and attention to detail. I also wish to thank three anonymous reviewers at the University of Michigan Press who helped me to clarify issues in the text.

Finally, I thank all the students in my linguistics classes during the past ten years who have asked probing questions about my examples of linguistic myths.

Contents

Introduction

Language fascinates and captivates. I have never met an adult who could not or would not talk about language. Everyone seems to have an opinion on language, dialects, and grammar, and few people seem interested in changing any of their linguistic opinions. When people find out that I am an English teacher (and a linguist), they feel free to tell me all sorts of things about language, yet they are never quite sure how they came to this knowledge, despite being steadfast in their opinion. They know, as do linguists, that language occupies a central place in our lives, and they cling tenaciously to their views about language and its role in society. Unfortunately, myths and misconceptions abound when it comes to language. Often what people tell me and what I see in the mainstream press are inaccurate, misleading, and, in the worst cases, dangerous.

In this book, I expose linguistic ideas that are held by the general public and even some educational policymakers. English as a second language (ESL) and mainstream teachers need to understand language so they can help shape better language policies on a variety of issues: bilingual education, non-standard dialects, accents, Ebonics, language change, slang, and the role of grammar in language education. These are perennial hot topics for educators, parents, and politicians and are commented on by countless pundits in the popular media, and these comments influence public opinion as well as teacher attitudes. The aim of this book is not to settle all language issues but rather to highlight popular linguistic fallacies and how they influence debates regarding language, and how these ultimately affect language policies in and out of the classroom.

The thesis of this book is simple: ESL teachers should work to debunk popular and misguided myths that dominate the general public's understanding of language. These myths are spread by the modern media and

1

ultimately have real-world repercussions in that they affect classroom practices and educational policies.

Popular (and uninformed) opinions on language exist.	+	Mass media repeats and disseminates the misconception.	=	Erroneous ESL policies are developed.

Linguists Laurie Bauer and Peter Trudgill (1999) question how language is so misunderstood today despite all that has been learned over the years about language and how it functions as a system. Somewhere there is a breakdown in the dissemination of linguistic knowledge and, unfortunately, the inaccurate opinions and reports are often more influential than the accurate ones. Bauer and Trudgill (1999) suggest the breakdown comes from people tuning out the esoteric works of professional linguists who rarely write for non-linguists. Like most professionals, linguists forget a general audience when they write. If we look at some of the best-selling books on language and linguistics—*The Story of English* (McCrum, MacNeil, & Cran, 1986), *The Mother Tongue* (Bryson, 2001), *Do You Speak American?* (MacNeil & Cran, 2005)—note that none were written by a linguist (Bauer & Trudgill, 1999). This is not to say that these books contain misleading information, only that they were not written by those who know the most about language. Because linguists are focused on conducting their own and keeping up with others' research, they lack time to write for non-linguists. So myths continue and are spread by "word of mouth" and, ultimately, some misconceptions reach the status of urban legends.

This book clarifies some of the most common myths about language and language acquisition, particularly those that affect ESL teachers and the decisions they make when they teach English language learners (ELL). These language issues are not relevant to only ESL teachers. They also apply to mainstream teachers given the fact that so many classrooms have not only ELLs but also dialect-minority students (native English speakers who use a non-standard dialect) in their classrooms. A reasonable case could be made that language is at the core of all education;

thus, there is a need for a clear understanding of language. This task of helping ELLs is becoming not only a responsibility of the ESL teacher, but all teachers because ELLs are becoming more prevalent in all schools and in all classes. The National Clearinghouse for English Language Acquisition notes that between 1995 and 2006, the number of ELLs grew 57.17 percent (2006). There is every indication that this trend will continue.

So what are some examples of language policies that adversely affect students and that have been prompted by an inaccurate understanding of language or language acquisition? One example concerns language restriction. In the early 1900s in the United States, the government imposed discriminatory policies that restricted the use of languages other than English. This was eventually a death sentence for many native American languages. This linguistic prohibition became particularly intense during the 1930s when Native American children were sent to boarding schools to "Americanize" them. The Americanizing process began with an effort to proscribe the use of any non-English language. To use a language other than English (even if the children were fluent in English) was considered an impediment to full enculturation into mainstream American society. Children would literally have their mouth washed out with soap if they used a Native American language on the playground.

Another example of linguistic prohibition in the United States happened during WWI and WWII, when speaking or even studying German in the United States was considered a sign of disloyalty. As a result, German as a foreign language was dropped from many college curricula. This sort of anti-German language sentiment reached its zenith with the passage in 1917 of the Babel Proclamation in Iowa, which prohibited the use of German in public. Iowa's governor, William Harding, deemed speaking German an affront to being American. He said:

> The official language of the United States and the state of Iowa is the English language. Freedom of speech is guaranteed by federal and state constitutions, but this is not a guarantee of the right to use a language other than the language of this country—the English language. (Quoted in Frese, 2005).

Restricting the use of languages other than English continues today in U.S. classrooms and, where possible, in society. In 2005, Supercuts®, the hair salon chain, was named in a lawsuit for implementing an English-only environment in which employees were reprimanded for speaking Spanish while they worked and during their breaks in the employee lounge. This policy was implemented in 22 Supercuts® stores in Chicago because it was deemed that speaking Spanish was, according to signs posted by managers at Supercuts®, "disrespectful" to customers (O'Connor, 2005).

The linguistic question here is this: Is it possible to legislate what language is spoken on the playground, studied at school, or spoken during a work break? There are no clear answers. What these examples do illustrate, however, is that language policies are implemented routinely in various contexts of human interaction: government, education, and business. And policies such as the Babel Act or that of Supercuts® were not as carefully considered. Being forbidden to use one's mother tongue can be frustrating and even traumatic. Classroom or school policies that forbid a language other than English can have devastating effects on ELLs because their language is denigrated.

While a ban on a language can certainly lead to problems, there can also be negative repercussions due to the use of a dialect (language variety) or accent (pronunciation) that leads to discrimination. In 1992, a Treasury Department official in Washington, DC, complained that a Filipino security guard was hard to understand. The result? Five Filipino security guards were all removed from their positions. There had been no other complaints, but a new *de facto* policy was implemented that required "native-like" accents. The security guards sued their employer to restore their "honor and dignity" under Title VII of the 1964 Civil Rights Act (which prohibits employers from discriminating against any individual "because of such individual's race, color, religion, sex, or national origin"), and the federal court recognized that this sort of language policy was discriminatory (Lippi-Green, 1997).

Policymakers (politicians, educators, and business owners) should understand language's fundamental role in human interaction as well as basic concepts about language before policies are implemented.

For example, research has consistently shown that school policies that strictly prohibit the use of a language other than English do more harm than good when it comes to a child's acquisition of English (Cummins, 2000). Policies that exclude languages or that denigrate minority English dialects give children the impression that their languages or dialects are inferior. ELLs and dialect-minority students are left with a choice: reject their home language or reject English-only policies. They are told that a rejection of English-only policies will slow their English acquisition, but this is not so. Affirming a child's native language or dialect in school settings increases acceptance and acquisition of standard English (Cummins, 2000; Krashen, 1996; Wolfram, Adger, & Christian, 1999). This is the sort of linguistic research that needs wider dissemination to counter the prevailing opinion that strict English-only policies are always sound policies. Unfortunately, linguistic insights do not always inform language policies and, as a result, detrimental language attitudes and policies persist.

To explain linguistic insights that are important for teachers, I will use a rhetorical strategy often used in religious services. Many religious leaders say that when they sermonize, they use two sources: a holy book and the newspaper. They try to relate profound theological ideas to everyday life. I will take a similar approach. I will "preach" some of the linguistic truths that have been discovered through research, and I will relate these to classrooms. I will present linguistic truths as well as how they are often misconstrued or simply ignored. My examples are drawn from newspapers, magazines, television shows, talk radio, and websites as well as personal conversations. These are the places where misconceptions are often spread. To be fair, there are articles in the press and popular media that accurately report on linguistic research; however, these articles will not be the focus in this book. Instead, the focus will be on the many reports that somehow get it wrong—the ones that distort information or leave out important parts and, in so doing, perpetuate misconceptions about language. The reports are not intentionally misleading; it is just that some myths and misconceptions about language are so entrenched that they surface in subtle and not so subtle ways. I highlight these quotes and news reports in sections titled **Media Spotlight**. Popular misconceptions about language thrive in all of these settings. The opinions of the general public are vigorously applied in shaping our language policies. This can be a good thing or a bad thing. I have mentioned some bad examples, such as policies that restrict other languages in work places or schools. However, sometimes public opinion can have positive results as when some words are deemed racially offensive and are eliminated, almost by consensus, from public discourse. When public opinion is grounded in language misconceptions, this can be dangerous and lead to unnecessary changes in parenting strategies, new ineffectual educational policy, and even the perpetuation of attitudes that border on being racist. Unquestionably, ESL and mainstream teachers are among those on the front line when it comes to language issues, so it is imperative that they develop a clear understanding of language.

School systems expect teachers (both ESL and mainstream) to perform many vital functions relating to ELLs, such as teaching them English grammar and helping them gain content knowledge. However, Nancy Hornberger (2002) of the University of Pennsylvania has said that *advocacy* is the most basic function of a teacher of ELLs. By this she meant that teachers must advocate for these students in a school system that, while not intentionally hostile, is at the very least an alien place for them. This advocacy entails shepherding students in an unfamiliar linguistic and cultural environment. This notion of advocacy needs to be taken a step further: Advocating for students also demands debunking linguistic misconceptions that lead to ill-formed policies that impede student success in U.S. schools. Teachers must be advocates for truth about language. Teacher advocacy can be as simple as explaining to administrators (and to the tax-weary public) how smaller class size for ESL classes aids acquisition, due to increased interaction with English, or explaining why strict English-only policies delay English acquisition. Administrators are not necessarily language experts, and teachers with a solid grasp of language can help them and other colleagues better understand language issues. Advocacy can also entail applying for educational grants for ESL programs and being able to articulate, based on research, how grant money can best be spent to aid ELLs.

Pre-service teachers in my classes who are new to the field of ESL often wonder why working with ELLs necessitates a background in linguistics. Some wonderful ESL teachers have enormous success in the classroom, yet they cannot tell a phoneme from a morpheme. However, while some linguistic terms may fade from these teachers' memories (Valdes, 2001), successful teachers understand language, and this understanding helps them when teaching verbs, idioms, and subject-verb agreement but also allows them to advocate for good language policies and raise their voice against detrimental ones.

While the spread of linguistic misconceptions continues, there is one piece of good news. Language has a life of its own. In spite of ill-formed policies based on false assumptions, language development continues, and students do acquire English. However, our uninformed linguistic tinkering may affect students' psyches, their attitudes toward learning English, and their academic success in an English environment, as this book will attest.

Humans develop their identity in and through language. We are not computers. We are emotional creatures, and developing a good sense of identity and belonging is key to emotional health. This sense of identity is intimately connected to language. We develop our identity in and through language. When someone criticizes our language or dialect, it is as though the attack is personal, and most people are quick to defend their own language and that of their community. Those who feel linguistically trampled will find vindication in the ideas presented in this book, I think.

The chapters of this book are organized by the topics and debates that are crucial around the world but in particular to the language/pedagogical situation in the United States. Chapter 1 provides some basic facts about language that are part of the canon of beliefs of linguists; however, many non-linguists disagree with them. While the assertions can and have been proven, they never seem to take root with the general public that is unaware of the research. There are too many erroneous stories in the news to indicate wide acceptance of these ideas. We develop ideas about people based on the clothes they wear, the way they walk, their hair style, and yes, the way they talk. We have heard time and again that certain varieties of English are better and are more correct. Some linguists collect editorials in newspapers written by members of the general public that decry the "bad" dialects of English (Graddol, Leith, & Swann, 1996; Aitchison, 1991). These editorials erroneously use words such as *corrupt* and *broken* to describe certain dialects. We judge people according to the variety of language they use. While language can reveal much about a person, it has its limitations, and when these limitations are ignored, we stereotype based on language.

Chapter 2 addresses the misconceptions related to learning a first language, which is of particular importance to parents and early child-hood educators. Parents want to do as much as possible to develop the language skills of their children, and teachers earnestly desire to continue this language development, but both groups often work under some illusions.

Chapter 3 confronts the myths about learning a second language. Since many adults and college graduates in the United States have taken a foreign language class, they have developed their own ideas about learning a second language. They have also listened to at least one or more foreign language teacher express his or her views on learning a new language. In my experience, foreign language teachers have often been the instigators when it comes to spreading misinformation about learning a second language.

Chapter 4 addresses how language and society interact. The chapter includes discussions about dialects and the movement in the United States to declare a national language. The possible movement to declare a national language is important for ESL teachers because they have opinions as to how such a law would affect ELLs.

Finally, Chapter 5 examines what we know about language and cognition. This is a complex and sometimes abstract topic and one that has its own sort of misconceptions. The questions addressed in the chapter include: How does language influence our thinking? Does "political correctness" prompt people to steer clear of discriminatory thinking through control of their language? Is swearing ruining language and our morality? yes!

Each chapter begins with a quote or quotes about language. These quotes introduce the topic of the chapter and also set a certain tone about the truths and myths that will be explored. Each chapter concludes with activities for teachers that give examples, exercises, or simple questions that relate directly to the ESL field and, in particular, to teachers' everyday dealings with ELLs and language. These activities are intended to stir reactions and be a focus for discussion and reflection about the issues presented in each chapter. A list of resources that may be useful for students and teachers in their quest to understand language follows.

There is one inherent danger in writing a book like this: spreading a false notion about language even as I attempt to clarify linguistic information. However, I am careful to point out research that supports my assertions.

Languages do indeed have a life of their own, but the attitudes we have toward languages profoundly influences what we think of those we hear speaking. Grammatical acumen is not a requirement for linguistic study, but serious self-reflection is. Despite being in the field of linguistics for a number of years, I too still fall prey to misconceptions. Despite how much I read and understand about language, I too sometimes make judgments that I know I should not. For instance, recently I went to a store to pick up film that I had left for processing and there was a problem with the film. I heard two of the film processors talking, and I hoped the one whose dialect I liked better would help me. After all, it meant he knew more about film . . . didn't it?

CHAPTER **1**

Myths about Language in General

Tongues, like governments, have a natural tendency to degeneration.

—Samuel Johnson, 1755

Language is not an abstract construction of the learned, or of dictionary makers, but is something arising out of the work, need, joys, affections, tastes, of long generations of humanity, and has its bases broad and low, close to the ground.

—Walt Whitman, 1888

The quotes represent two dichotomous views in a fundamental and long-standing debate regarding language. Samuel Johnson, an eighteenth-century lexicographer, intimates that language can degenerate. This represents a common and somewhat alarmist opinion about language that was not only prevalent in Johnson's time but is in fact still prevalent now. The alarm that Johnson sounded—and that some still think is true—is that English will degenerate into an incoherent mess. On the other end of the linguistic spectrum is poet Walt Whitman. Whitman's opinion, and likely that of most dictionary writers today, is that language usage arises from the people and is "close to the ground." Degeneration did not enter his estimation of language, and he did not sound an alarm if language changed. Rather, he focused on the language of the people and what the people in the street used.

The misconceptions that will be discussed in this chapter are:

1. Some languages and dialects are better than others.
2. Grammar usage reflects a person's moral character.
3. Languages and dialects are determined by race.
4. Languages have one correct form, and this form should not change.

> ❶ **Misconception:** Some languages and dialects are better than others.
>
> **Truth:** From a grammatical, communicative, and aesthetic perspective, all languages are equal.

Linguist William Mackey wrote: "Only before God and the linguist are all languages equal" (1978, p. 7). The reality is that no one language is better than another. Languages have several functions: they allow us to communicate, they help us think, and they situate us in speech communities (O'Grady, Archibald, Aronoff, Rees-Miller, 2005, p. 1). (Pullum and Scholz define speech community as "a human group whose members broadly understand each other's speech and recognize it as being characteristic of the group" [2001, p. 367].)

If these are indeed the primary functions of language, then all languages must be equal because all languages allow their speakers to communicate and identify with groups (Fromkin, Rodman, & Hyams, 2006). Every language has different words to name and describe objects and actions. And, certainly, the world's languages differ in grammatical structure. Some languages such as English use definite articles (e.g., *the*, *a*), while other languages such as Russian rarely use them. Some languages like Spanish use many prepositions, while others, such as Latin, use very few. These lexical and grammatical differences, however, do not imply superiority or inferiority; superior or inferior status is a label that people ascribe to languages.

Equality in Grammar

Language equality is not universally understood or accepted. Those who report on language topics for the media also do not understand this and so sometimes make inaccurate statements about language in their stories. I am not implying that it is the media's job to promulgate all linguistic facts. Rather, I simply am drawing attention to the fact that many people (including teachers) find their erroneous notions about language confirmed by inaccurate or incomplete statements that appear in the press. Consider this report about Latin in schools: *Time* magazine ran an article about a school district in Fairfax, Virginia, that was using Latin to help middle schoolers grasp the grammatical structure of English (Eskenazi, 2000). Test scores improved as did students' grasp of English grammar, but there is one troubling line in the article:

☼ Media Spotlight

And once kids master the grammatical structure of Latin—which is simple, logical, and consistent—they will more easily grasp the many grammatical exceptions in English (Eskenazi, 2000, p. 61).

The truth is that Latin is not more "simple, logical, and consistent" than English. If you have ever tried to memorize all those inflections (word endings) in Latin, you know the grammar is not simple. English is not simple either. It does not have as many inflections as Latin does, but it does depend on a strict set of rules for syntax (word order). There is a balance in the world's languages: some languages depend more on inflections, and some depend more on word order (Searchinger, 1994). If a second language learner goes from one kind of language to another, then it seems like the other is quite complex or more logical (or illogical). It's all perspective.

Examples of languages that tend toward an inflectional system (languages that depend more on word endings) and examples of languages that tend toward an analytic system (languages that depend more on word order) are shown. Of course, languages fall somewhere on the continuum between being inflected or analytic, but this gives examples of languages that tend toward inflectional or analytic.

Inflected Languages		
Latin	French	Irish
German	Spanish	French

Analytic Languages		
English	Afrikaans	Swedish
Chinese	Japanese	Finnish

In his 2006 book *The Ultimate Gift: How Children of the World Learn and Unlearn the Language of the World,* linguist Charles Yang makes a tongue-in-cheek argument for the superiority of the Turkish language. He wryly contends that if the superiority of languages depends on the complexity of the inflectional system (an argument many make in favor of Latin), then perhaps we should enshrine Turkish as the model language since it is a much richer language in terms of inflections than Latin. His argument illustrates the subjective nature of comparing languages in terms of grammatical superiority.

What the *Time* story was trying to say was that there's a benefit to learning Latin. The implication that it is a "perfect" language is the problem. In fact, the benefit derives from comparing English with Latin. In this sense, any language would work because students would be able to compare one grammatical structure with another. They would be forced to learn terms such as noun, verb, and direct object when they compare the two and thus be able to see and appreciate English grammar. Obviously, there is the added benefit that many English academic words have Latinate origins. So studying Latin *is truly beneficial:* it helps with grammatical understanding and vocabulary. However, it does not serve as an example of a perfect language to which all languages and students should strive.

The Virginia school district might have chosen Spanish and had the same results, plus the added benefit of students being able to use the language in real-life settings with a growing Latino population. It all depends on the aims of the language program as to which language should be studied.

Educators in Fort Wayne, Indiana, reported that students who studied Latin scored better on tests than those that did not (Roduta, 2003). However, the report did not note if students who did not study Latin studied another foreign language. Perhaps those students studied no foreign language at all. So it might not have been Latin itself but just the fact that students were exposed to a foreign language. It may be that the students scoring higher are studying a foreign language and that many are studying Latin, and that the results are skewed accordingly.

Of course, no harm is done by studying Latin. But if students inadvertently pick up the message that one language is better than another, then what is to stop students from saying English is better than Spanish? Seeds for discrimination are sown based on this attitude. The result may be that some people think their language is not on equal standing with other languages, that their language is either superior or inferior. A friend told me that she once talked to a mother who had to select a second language for her high school student to study. The choices were French or Spanish. The mother explained that she chose French because Spanish is the language of "all those poor people." Obviously not everyone believes all languages are equal. This mother certainly did not, and it is painfully obvious by her remark that, unfortunately, she associated the Spanish language with "poor people."

Equality in Communicative Capability

What about the ability to communicate? Even if some languages are not superior in a grammatical sense, are some in a communicative sense? Are not some languages better because they are more expressive? Texas's Ma Ferguson, our nation's first female governor, remarked with regard to bilingual studies in 1920, "If the King's English was good enough for Jesus, it's good enough for me!" (as cited in Safire, 1984, p. 265). Whether quipped in jest or in sincerity, these kinds of comments and attitudes (not based on facts) influence people's perception of language. Some people think that certain languages just do a better job of communicating because they have been told that Latin (or Greek or French) is better for certain tasks such as drawing up a treaty or writing a novel.

Ma Ferguson's quote is assumed to be a defense of the communicative capacity of English; this is not the first time a language has been defended for its ability to communicate, but the truth is all languages have equal ability to express any feeling, thought, or idea (Fromkin, Rodman, & Hyams, 2006, p. 28). It cannot be otherwise. Just because a certain language has a more developed vocabulary in a certain area does not mean that it has more communicative ability. Other languages can and will develop that vocabulary if needed. For example, since many computer innovations originated in the United States, English developed an extensive vocabulary that dealt with computers. However, as computer technology expanded, other languages quickly developed their own vocabulary. Sometimes words were taken from English and pronunciation was altered to fit the language; at other times, it was the speakers who developed their own computer terminology. For example, Spanish has adopted the word *email* with a Spanish pronunciation and it also has the phrase *correo electrónico* for email as well. Both the loan word and the new phrase are used. Languages are able to adapt to allow speakers to express themselves.

When I was in college, my philosophy professor said that the reason the ancient Greeks wrote so much philosophy was that the Greek language had so many verbs and was thus better equipped to express philosophical ideas. He went on to say that English was a poor language for philosophy because it had so few verbs, and that English had no equivalent for many of the Greek verbs. I was intrigued and bewildered. If this were true, then I could never truly master philosophy; I could not learn Greek because there were all those verbs that could not be translated into English. How could anybody learn Greek as a second language? My professor was American. How did he learn Greek with all those extra verbs that could not be translated?

Even then I suspected something must be wrong with this statement. Later I learned that English, or any language, could develop the verbs (or any words) if it needed to; it could be just as "philosophical" as Greek. If there is a need for new words or a new nuance of meaning, a language will develop. For example, when English-speaking colonists arrived in America, they borrowed heavily from Native American languages, which provided names for much of the flora and fauna that were new to the colonists: *hickory, chipmunk, opossum,* and *squash* (Fromkin, Rodman, & Hyams, 2006, p. 476). More recently, English has added words that deal with technology: *blog, net, texting.* This is evidence that "membership in the word stock of a natural language is open" (Pullum & Scholz, 2001, p. 367). Languages constantly add new words to fit new situations.

Equality in Beauty

Even if it can be agreed that languages are equal in grammar and in communicative ability, many of my linguistics students have said that they are unequal in beauty. How can anyone critique someone else's judgments of beauty? You can no more tell people that their appreciation of the sound of one language over another is unfounded than you can tell people that their love of Mozart over Elvis Presley is without foundation. However, we can draw attention to the fact that our preferences are entirely subjective and have nothing to do with objective linguistic reality.

Linguists Howard Giles and Nancy Niedzielski have proposed that we should not fight the battle to purge aesthetic judgments when it comes to language. Instead,

> we should encourage teachers and others not to abandon these judgments entirely but to recognize them for what they are: the result of a complex of social, cultural, regional, political and personal associations and prejudices. Most listeners know of linguistic varieties that they do not like, but we should appreciate that these feelings are highly subjective and have no basis in social scientific fact. In particular, such feelings should not be allowed to influence teachers', the media's and politicians' attitudes and policies towards children's and others' language varieties. (1998, p. 92)

Being aware of these prejudices is important.

Hollywood often perpetuates notions that some languages are more beautiful. In the movie *A Fish Called Wanda* (1988), Jamie Lee Curtis' character loves it when her boyfriend (played by Kevin Kline) speaks Italian. In fact, it stirs her passions, and this is a constant source of humor in the movie. But the fact is, neither Kevin Kline nor his character speak Italian. All he is able to say are memorized phrases like *Dove il Vaticano?* (Where's the Vatican?) or *Dove il bano?* (Where's the bathroom?). In actuality, the sounds of Italian or any other language are not inherently more pleasing. It is what we associate with those languages and their sounds that make them so. If Italian stirs passions, it is not the consonants, vowels, or intonation pattern; it is, rather, associations with that language. Many claim that the sounds of German are harsh. But harsh is a subjective term. Are German babies distressed when they hear German sounds coming from their mother? Hardly. They are comforted because mom is near and is speaking to them. But the sounds and structures of different languages are simply that: sounds and structures. They are not inherently beautiful or ugly. The task of language specialists then is to make educational policymakers aware of the unscientific judgments about the grammatical and communicative capabilities of other languages as well as the highly subjective nature of aesthetic judgments of languages. This will allow language policies to be based on fact.

Equality in Dialect Variation

Throughout history and all over the world, people have made judgments about dialects (varieties of a language that are mutually intelligible) and accents (pronunciation features of dialects). Some examples of situations in which judgments are made based on dialects follow.

☼ Media Spotlight

In his speech the mountaineer touches a very remote past ... The mountaineer simply keeps in use old words and meanings that the valley people have ceased to use. . . . There are perhaps two hundred words, meanings, and pronunciations that are in the mountaineer's speech that go back unchanged to Chaucer.

"Talk of the Southern Mountaineer,"
New York Times, 1901

Linguist John Baugh has conducted research based on phone inquiries about rental property using an African-American accent, a Latino accent, and a standard American accent. His results show accent discrimination against the African-American and Latino accent.

(Purnell, Idsardi, & Baugh, 1999)

Although individuals with different dialects should not be penalized, this research ... indicates that such penalty does exist in hiring. [Job] recruiters who state that they do not discriminate on the basis of race, color, sex, religion, age, national origin, or handicap seem to be discriminating on the basis of nonstandard dialect.

(Atkins, 1993)

According to Preston (1999), some Americans hold negative judgments about some dialects of English (the southern dialect is inferior, New Yorkers have an abrasive dialect, the Latino accent is lazy sounding) and positive judgments about other dialects (the Midwest dialect of American English is standard, the British dialect is authoritative, the Irish dialect is quaint, a French accent in English is prestigious).

Writers capitalize on dialect features in novels, and directors use dialects in movies in order to add authenticity to their stories and help the audience size up characters. Directors use non-standard dialects for certain characters to show place of origin or to imply something about the character. Unfortunately, the use of dialects in novels and movies can perpetuate inaccurate stereotypes of certain dialects and lend credence to the notion of dialect or accent superiority. For example, the southern American English dialect can be portrayed as substandard and incorrect and, based on this, there is an association that anyone who speaks this dialect is less intelligent, superstitious, and of a lower class (Lippi-Green, 1997).

What makes the study of people's unsubstantiated judgments about dialects a particularly fascinating area of language inquiry is the fervor with which groups and individuals cling to their false notions of dialects. Dennis Preston's dialect surveys reveal that even some Southerners think the southern dialect is substandard and inferior, and they develop a sort of "linguistic self-hatred." They also consider the sounds of this dialect beautiful and integral to southernness.

The fact is that dialects arise due to either geographic or social distance. As languages change, groups who speak the same language but are separated by geography or social class will develop different features because of this distance. When two varieties of a language have enough distinguishing features (while maintaining mutual intelligibility), new dialects have developed. Multiple dialects of a language are in competition to be considered the standard.

This competition also occurs at many levels. Sometimes a local dialect has great prestige and social currency in the local area. This could be termed covert prestige and sometimes develops in resistance to a national standard. For example, in the United States, we have any number of prestigious local dialects. Andy Griffith's dialect in the television comedy *The Andy Griffith Show* is a good example. The actor is a native of North Carolina and in the early seasons of the show, Griffith utilizes an Appalachian dialect, pronouncing *on* with an /o/ (versus standard English, which uses /a/ like the vowel in *opposite*). He says *eggs* with an initial vowel of /e/, which sounds like the final vowel sound in *they*. In the early seasons, he often uses *they is* for *there is*. These examples illustrate distinctive features of this dialect, which is very important in Appalachia. However, producers for *The Andy Griffith Show* (and Andy Griffith himself) decided to change his dialect after the first two seasons. The show was broadcast around the country, and the producers were concerned that the distinctly Appalachian dialect would alienate too much of the country that considered this dialect inferior (Kelly, 1981).

Linguistically, there is nothing less systematic nor less expressive about an Appalachian dialect when compared to a northern or west coast dialect. It is society's perception that makes a dialect seem inferior. Dialects are equal, and one dialect becomes the standard not because it is better, but because of forces outside the language itself. People take the next step, assuming a standard is *better* instead of correctly identifying that it simply carries more social currency.

When the 1964 movie *Mary Poppins* was released, there was criticism of Dick Van Dyke's Cockney accent. Van Dyke's attempt at the Cockney dialect illustrates that people are at some level aware that we all have dialects and when we cross into using another dialect, we move into someone else's territory. And no matter how perfectly we use this other dialect, we are subject to being looked at with suspicion. Dialects help define our particular group, and we do not want our dialect to be considered inferior or the object of ridicule, but many people have no hesitation in ridiculing other dialects. This ridicule is always based on the notion that there is a dialectless version of a language. It is not surprising that those who ridicule say they have no dialect, but everyone else does.

Implications for Teachers

Assuming some languages or dialects to be superior to others poses a pedagogical pitfall: ESL and mainstream teachers may unconsciously make assumptions about their ELLs' scholastic ability based on the students' native language. There is a danger in assuming that students are more or less intelligent based on the native languages. If a teacher thinks that certain languages or dialects are superior to others, then he or she may unintentionally have lower expectations for the students who speak a more "inferior" language. For example, I have had teachers tell me that Mexican students do not speak "real" Spanish. These teachers maintain that the Spanish of Mexico is impure and nothing like Castilian Spanish. Ironically, many of these teachers are not speakers of Spanish. The concern is that the misconception will inevitably negatively affect their expectations of the students who speak a Mexican dialect of Spanish.

Implications for Teachers

Another implication of this myth is that many ELLs in the United States come from countries where there is a strong tradition of British English. These students often look down on American English and think that the real English is British. Teachers must work with these students to gently convince students that American English is just as valid as British English, and in America, British English, while prestigious, is marked and may not always be appropriate.

---

❷ **Misconception:** Grammar usage reflects a person's moral character.
Truth: Use of non-standard grammar does not reveal moral depravity.

"Six hundred years ago, every rustic knew, that is to say practiced daily, perfections and niceties in the German language of which the best grammarians nowadays do not even dream (Jakob Grimm, quoted in Yang, 2006, p. 181). Jakob Grimm (of the Brothers Grimm's fairytale fame) studied languages and discovered one of historical linguistics' best-known laws about language change in the Indo-European languages (a group of language families that includes English), now known as Grimm's Law. Grimm's Law explains the sound shifts in Germanic languages that differentiate Germanic languages from other Indo-European languages. Despite his expertise in **philology,** Grimm's word *niceties* seems to indicate that he equated good manners with good grammar, which even today is a rather common misunderstanding about language.

Some people contend that speaking a certain way or using "correct" (linguists prefer the word *standard*) grammar is essential to having good moral values. Consider these quotes on language and morality.

- Bishop Lowth, an eighteenth-century grammarian and churchman, noted that to deviate from correct grammar was to displease God (Graddol et al., 1996, p. 161).
- Walter Williams, a radio commentator, said, "Listening to how English is spoken nowadays is one more indicator of our decline in values and standards" (2000).

- In 1996, British Secretary of Education Gillian Shepard announced the Better English Campaign. Many applauded the campaign because of general concern about lack of proper behavior by English youth. In other words, there was an association between proper English and proper behavior (Marshall, 1996).
- Abraham Clearfield, a minister in College Station, Texas, commented that children must be raised with the Ten Commandments as well as be taught proper English (Clearfield, 2005).

These quotes imply that to not speak a certain way is to not have good moral values. This is a common notion regarding English and other languages. The more people listen to "bad grammar" in any language, the more they feel that such ill-formed grammar constructions reveal a moral decline. Grammar of course does not reveal moral virtue or moral turpitude. Nonetheless, it is difficult not to make personal judgments about someone who speaks what we consider non-standard English.

The unsubstantiated link between good grammar and a stable society is the source of many editorials. Newspapers often run stories and editorials on why "correct" grammar promotes this stability. There were several such stories after Gilles de Robien, France's education minister, unveiled plans to implement a new curricular policy in 2007 based on teaching more traditional grammar. Robien claimed such grammar lessons would curb youth violence by teaching the youth to think and express themselves more clearly, which would lead to less frustration and more constructive dialogue with authority, thus avoiding a recurrence of the riots that occurred in France in 2005 (Marshall, 2006). Certainly having good grammar does not prevent violence or social decay.

People who argue that good grammar promotes more stability will agree that adherence to grammar rules means adherence to rules in general, including moral ones. But what about those who have had little exposure to standard English grammar? Should they be suspected of moral laxity? People attach all sorts of beliefs about language to the person who speaks it, but doing so is like judging a person by his or her clothes. A person's taste in fashion reveals something about the person, but it is hard to make judgments of morality based on such taste.

Implications for Teachers

Judging students' ability to follow the rules based on whether their grammar is "correct" may lead some teachers not to trust certain students or to avoid giving them leadership positions. Whether students lack good grammar because of their educational background, family background, or their status as non–native English speakers, teachers should keep in mind that conformity to standard grammatical rules is not a determiner of students' character. Conformity to standard grammar is expected for many jobs, and this should be emphasized, but teachers must guard against judging students who do not conform to these grammatical standards.

---

❸ **Misconception:** Languages and dialects are determined by race.
Truth: Any person from any racial background can learn any language.

Race is a sensitive subject in the United States. The one issue that is rarely addressed in discussions about race is language, but it should be included because there are misconceptions about race and language: most notably that a person's ethnicity determines their language and dialect. Here is a fundamental truth about language: One's race or ethnicity does not determine his or her language, dialect, or accent. Each of us is born with the ability to speak any language and any dialect. As time goes on and as we mature, we are limited more to the languages and dialects that we hear regularly. Ethnicity has no bearing in a physical sense, although race can segregate English speakers into groups, causing dialect differences (Fromkin, Rodman, & Hyams, 2006, p. 410).

There have been those who maintain that languages are linked to race. In 1969, psychologist Arthur Jensen published an article in the *Harvard*

Education Review in which he proposed that African Americans lacked the intellectual ability to acquire Standard English. Linguists since then have pointed out the serious flaws in his arguments, but there are those who still agree with this position. Today, mainstream publications are careful not to publish anything that perpetuates this myth, but it exists in the minds of people today. This myth, perhaps more than any other language myth, must be shattered because it perpetuates racist and bigoted thinking, and may affect teachers' work with students.

The informal idea that race determines language is most often associated with the dialect known as African-American English (AAE), which is also sometimes referred to as Ebonics. There is no question that this dialect exists, but if it is not related to ethnicity, how does it come to be? Theories abound ranging from a mixing of West African linguistic elements to isolation due to slavery. The key, whatever the origin, is that this language variety is maintained because it offers solidarity to its speakers, not because it is linked to race. As Toni Morrison has said, "The language, only the language. . . . It is the thing that black people love so much . . . It's a love, a passion. . . . The worst of all possible things that could happen would be to lose that language" (1981, qtd in Fromkin, Rodman, & Hyams, 2006, p. 423).

This is why some African Americans speak AAE and some do not. Some want to "sound black," and others resist because this particular dialect is perceived as non-standard in the United States. African Americans may be chastised by other African Americans because they are trying to "sound white" if they do not use this dialect. This is strong criticism, but it is a social issue and not a physiological issue. In addition, AAE is not restricted to the African-American community and is in fact spoken by many others outside that community. In fact, many English words have their origins in West Africa and crossed into mainstream English from AAE. Among them are *tote* and *nitty gritty*. Though it is highly disputed, McCrum, MacNeil, and Cran (1986) even attribute *okay* to West Africa.

AAE is not linked to any race in a physiological sense. Consider this: How is it possible that an African-American child raised in a predominately white area can produce English that has no features of AAE? This would not be possible if language were strictly linked to genetics and physiology. Also, how could a white child learn this dialect if it were related to genetics? He or she could not.

AAE became an issue during the O.J. Simpson trial when a neighbor of Simpson testified that on the night in question, he heard a "black man speaking." From this witness's angle, he could not see the speaker; he only heard the voice. Immediately, Johnnie Cochran, Simpson's lawyer, objected to this testimony and stated that it had long been established that you could not tell race by someone's dialect. Inherently, dialect has no relationship to race. However, dialect is related to socialization and fitting in with a group (O'Grady, Archibald, Aronoff, & Rees-Miller, 2005, p. 492). Dialect is not determined by race, but each of us, because of our race, selects a certain dialect. We want to speak like those around us, and we want to identify with them. So if a speaker has an AAE dialect, there is a very good chance he or she is African American, but not necessarily.

The Oakland Resolution on Ebonics

A famous Ebonics resolution in Oakland, California, in 1996 sought to assist African-American students by acknowledging their home "language" even as the school sought to help students acquire standard English. There was an outcry around the country once the media began to cover the issue.

Based on the media coverage, it appeared that the Oakland schools would be teaching Ebonics when, in fact, the plan was to acknowledge Ebonics and use it as a bridge to standard English. The stated goal was to improve student test scores by improving students' command of standard English. Equally controversial was the Oakland School Board's resolution that used the word *genetic* in relation to language—an unfortunate choice of words. What the board meant was that languages may be genetically related: Spanish, Portuguese, and French are all related because they have the same origin, Latin. In the same way, the school board in

Oakland was saying that AAE was genetically related to languages in West Africa. However, people understood this use of the word in the resolution to mean that African Americans are genetically pre-disposed to Ebonics.

When the resolution was published, people from all walks of life had opinions about AAE and its role in education and in society. Jesse Jackson condemned the 1996 Ebonics resolution calling it "an unacceptable surrender, bordering on disgrace" (Knapp, 1996). Author Shelby Steele (2006) contended that recognition of Ebonics is nothing more than "white guilt" and an attempt to appease black Americans. Bill Cosby inflamed members of the African American community when he weighed in on AAE:

> I can't even talk the way these people talk: "Why you ain't?" "Where you is?" . . . And I blamed the kid until I heard the mother talk. And then I heard the father talk. . . . Everybody knows it's important to speak English except these knuckleheads. . . . You can't be a doctor with that kind of crap coming out of your mouth! (Quoted in Coates, 2004)

The pedagogical question remains, does recognizing and validating someone's home dialect foster or impede progress toward mastery of the standard? Language is too personal to be denigrated and for there not to be repercussions. An African-American student who feels the school system is putting down his or her dialect will react negatively so that acknowledging and validating one's home dialect does help students when they study standard English. Oakland tried to address the issue of home dialect while still promoting standard English; this was the school's stated intention.

Linguists understand that dialects are simply window dressing. They are not corruptions. Dialects serve a communicative and social purpose. Linguists (Labov, 1972; Aitchison, 1991; Wolfram, 1999) have been saying this for a long time, but the message is slow to be accepted by the general public as evidenced by the amount of controversy surrounding the Ebonics debate.

Implications for Teachers

If teachers hold the view that race and language are linked, this perception may prejudice them against certain students. This prejudice affects not only African-American students but ELLs as well. A teacher may consciously or unconsciously hold a view that certain races are less capable of learning standard English. Of course, most teachers would not hold this view, but teachers must be vigilant in challenging views that perpetuate this kind of thinking, especially when it influences educational policy. Valdes (2001) reports that teachers in her study had the view that Chinese students could master English more quickly than Mexican students. As a result, Chinese students exited ESL programs faster and were placed in mainstream classes. There are many reasons why Chinese students may have exited more quickly, but it must not be assumed that Chinese students were just better at languages. Teachers must challenge administrative and program decisions that hinder language acquisition. They must also help their colleagues who hold more antiquated views on language and language acquisition.

---

❹ **Misconception:** Languages have one correct form, and this form should not change.
Truth: Every language has a standard form; no language has one "correct" and immutable form.

The word *correct* is problematic for linguists when they discuss language. Linguists never use this word; it is taboo. *Standard* is the preferred term. We all want our children to speak and write well. Articulate speech and sophisticated written prose have benefits and are a requirement in most parts of our society. Educators teach it, employers expect it, and parents demand it. A common English standard is useful, but what is the difference between *correct* language and *standard* language? Correct language implies an objective verifiable standard, but language cannot be verified in this way. Can a "correct" form be proved scientifically? If it could, then we would use the word *correct* because there is a scientifically proven "right form." If not, then we must use the word *standard* when discussing language because this implies that people agree on what is the standard. People determine what will be considered standard, and this is done in conscious and unconscious ways.

If someone wants to retain the word *correct* with regard to linguistic structure, then who decides what is "correct"? Many parents and teachers would respond that something is correct if it is in a dictionary or grammar book. But who writes the grammar books? The answer is people. Dictionaries and grammar books are written by individuals and publishers, based on what is currently accepted in speech and written discourse. The writers of dictionaries and grammar books do not determine usage; dictionaries and grammar books reflect what is already being used.

Linguists are often criticized on this point because, to the average person, linguists seem to say that just about anything is standard. As Walt Wolfram, a sociolinguist, says with regard to standard language, "No one is suggesting that this [non-standard] structure should be considered standard English, just that its linguistic integrity stands apart from its social assessment" (Bauer & Trudgill, 1999, p. 109). Wolfram is noting that language cannot be incorrect because its ability to perform its intended task is not enhanced by a subjective notion of being correct. Language cannot be broken or incorrect, but we can label all sorts of varieties as non-standard. There is no authoritative correct version because people are arbitrarily deciding what is correct.

Here is a simple but illustrative example of debate surrounding language correctness. The word *disrespect* is a perfectly standard word when used as a noun, but what about when used as a verb? Notice the usage in an article from *People*, an entertainment magazine:

≳●≲   Media Spotlight

The government (in China) is still angry that *Red Corner*, the 1997 drama costarring Bai Ling and Richard Gere that was critical of the Chinese judicial system, was timed to be released in the U.S. during the visit of President Jiang Zemin. Ling, 31, now an American citizen who lives in Los Angeles, has apologized, saying in *People* that it was never her intention to **disrespect** China (Cunneff, 2002).

If you consult grammar manuals, you will find that this usage of *disrespect* is growing in acceptance. Its status as standard or non-standard depends on the person writing the grammar book. Some maintain that it is incorrect to use *disrespect* as a verb. But it is regularly being used this way, and there is very little a language purist (a person who believes language has one correct form) can do to stop it. The debate on this word has ended because it has grown in acceptance by so many, but there will always be language debates on usage. Two hundred years ago, Thomas Jefferson was ridiculed for his usage of the word *belittle*. At the time, it was not accepted, but now it is. This illustrates that it is difficult to use language correctness because there will always be debates on what is correct.

The Spanish and the French both have language academies (in Spain and France, respectively) to answer questions of standard, but American English has no such academy. To fill this void, we look to dictionaries as guardians of the standard. Yet, there is a controversy every time a new edition of a dictionary is published. Some lament the inclusion of slang (words that are considered non-standard). What are dictionary publishers to do? If the words are in use, they have an obligation to reflect that, despite criticism from language purists of promoting "incorrect English." The *Oxford English Dictionary* (OED) now includes words such as *doh* (Homer Simpson's catch phrase), *Bollywood* (the film industry in India), and *full monty* ("to go naked").

A good example of how the inclusion of certain words is controversial is the word *McJob*, which the *Merriam-Webster Dictionary* included and defined as "a low-paying job that requires little skill and provides little opportunity for advancement." McDonald's® CEO complained to Merriam-Webster claiming that such a word demeaned all those who worked in the restaurant industry. However, the word exists in the language and is being used, so lexicographers included it. Lexicographers do not decide whether a word is "correct" or not, but they can mark it as standard or non-standard. *Mcjob* may not be standard anymore than *doh* is, but using the word *standard* instead of *correct* highlights the subjective nature of language decisions.

There is another group of words that enter into languages and initially cause some angst. These are eponyms, words that are brand names, but are now also standard words. *Coke, Xerox, Kleenex,* and even *zipper* are good examples. They are used in general speech and no longer only mean the brand names. While it may be "incorrect" to use them outside of their proper noun status, people now do. Eble (1996) published a book on the slang of college students. Which do you consider non-standard? Will any of these reach the level of being standard?

Other Controversial Words: Which do you consider non-standard?		
wasted (drunk)	granola (a natural life-style)	hot (attractive)
ace (to do well)	chill (relax)	pig out (eat quickly)

From Eble, C. (1996). *Slang and sociability: In-group languages among college students.* Chapel Hill, NC: University of North Carolina Press.

It is not just words that are problematic when we discuss standards; it also is usage. Robert Byrd, the long-time senator from West Virginia, lamented from the Senate floor about the use of English among the young. His examples of *like* (as a quotative) and *you know* were meant to elicit great passion on how our language was declining and how we needed to get back to the "correct" way of speaking. But correct is problematic when describing language, but there are constant reports in the media about how language is falling into terminal disrepair.

> ### ⊰●⊱   Media Spotlight
>
> Brian Williams and *NBC Nightly News* ran a short story on the "pitiful" state of our language on the November 11, 2005 broadcast. What was intriguing was the assumption of the deterioration of English. The story goes on to profile a "few brave people" who are standing up against this degeneration of correct English. But what the story did not report was that people have always lamented a perceived downward spiral in English. They reported it as if it were news and only a recent event. The debate has existed for generations (Reise, 2001).

One example from the past is the British Poet Laureate Robert Bridges, who came to the United States in 1924 to promote the newly formed Society for Pure English. The Society's explicit aim was to protect English from changes that were deemed "incorrect." One of the areas that he wanted to clean up was pronunciation that, according to Bridges, "had gotten sloppy." He wanted to preserve the "richness of differentiation in our vocabulary, grammatical usages, and traditional idioms . . . while opposing whatever is slipshod and careless" (Pope, 1924).

Notions of language correctness always necessitate a discussion of language change. Change in any language is inevitable, but that does not mean everyone likes it. When it comes to change in language, most fear it or, at the very least, think that change in a language means that language is getting worse. To complicate matters, this change has religious and moral implications for some. But language change is not good or bad. It does not prove moral corruption; it just happens.

First, languages are always changing, and we cannot stop them from changing. We can call it "butchering" or "contamination" if we like, but it is neither. Change is a completely natural process in language and not a degenerative one. The Queen's English (spoken by only 10 percent of England's population) is often regarded as preserving a pure form of English and resisting any degenerative change. However, some supposed alterations, such as the American preference for *gotten (He has gotten drunk every night this week)* (instead of the British preference *got*) are actually older forms. We conserved this one; the British lost it, but the perception on both sides of the Atlantic is that Americans change English while the British preserve it. The reality is English changes in both countries.

Other examples to illustrate that change is simply a fact of life for language are:

- People criticize AAE speakers for saying *aks* instead of *ask*. However, the form of the word in Chaucer's time was *aks*. So should we abandon our modern-day standard of *ask* because it is a change from "the original"? Few would lobby for this, though it is an older form.

- The word *edit* was not an accepted word for a long time. The word *editor* existed but not *edit*. Mistakenly people assumed the /er/ sound at the end of *editor* was like the /er/ sound on the end of *teacher* or *player,* so they started using the word *edit* in the same way as *teach* and *play*. But it was a mistake because the ending of *editor* that sounds like the *–er* ending was an accidental occurrence. This method of creating a new word is known as back formation (creating a new word from a shortened form of an existing word), and we can be sure there was someone saying that using the word *edit* was a change for the worse. Now our language could hardly exist without the word *edit*. Language changed to meet a growing communicative need.

This debate about language change is not new. In 1927, the British Board of Film Censors issued an ultimatum to the nascent American film industry. They were not upset at the vulgarity and immorality in movies—that was still a few decades away. The ultimatum dealt with the English subtitles for silent movies that the British Board vowed to censor until the subtitles were rendered into "good English before the picture would be exhibited before British audiences" (Orman, 1927). With the advent of "talkies" in the 1930s, there was an even more urgent sense on the part of the British to protect English from changes from the United States. Here are two quotes that reveal a growing sense of this urgency and dread of change in English influenced by American talking movies:

- The words and accent are perfectly disgusting, and there can be no doubt that such films are an evil influence on our society (Sir Alex Knox, 1930, qtd. in Bragg, 2004).
- Those truly loathsome transatlantic importations—[words and expressions like] *to help make, worth-while, nearby,* and *colourful*—are spreading like the plague (*Daily Telegraph,* 1935, qtd. in Bragg).

Talking movies added to the sense in England that American English was invading, and as a result, we were butchering English. The truth is that language was changing in Great Britain and in the United States. While changes in language will happen, reactions to it remain remarkably stable: shock, annoyance, and even anger.

Once we dispense with the notion that language change is language degeneration, we are left with two opposing forces that result in language change. One is the social networking. People will change their language to fit in with a certain group. It is the social networking (wanting to be included in certain groups or, conversely, to distance from other groups) that causes people to alter language use, and this in turn nudges language to change. Another force is that such socially generated changes may cause a disruption to a system. The language system then tries to repair itself but, in so doing, may cause further systematic disruptions. As Aitchinson notes, "The two opposing pulls are an essential characteristic of language." These "opposing pulls" are very strong, and even an institutions as the Royal French Academy has had very little success in regulating language or proscribing certain changes.

Implications for Teachers

Teachers have an enormous responsibility to teach standard English. Their students will need to have competence in standard English to succeed in college and in the workforce. Yet, young students do not always see the relevance of learning standard English. They often seem to think more about fitting in with peers than they think about future employment. As Wolfram says, "The factor that is probably most responsible for success (or lack of it) in teaching someone to speak a standard dialect is relevance. People are motivated to learn a dialect that is relevant to their lives" (1999, p. 114). This is when dialoguing with students about standards and correctness is crucial. If a teacher approaches the language question by using standard versus non-standard terminology instead of correct versus incorrect, students may feel as though their dialect is not being denigrated and may be more open to seeing the relevance of standard English. Teachers can approach the issue by showing examples of when it is appropriate to use standard English and when non-standard usage may be important. This applies to non-standard dialect users as well as ELLs.

Implications for Teachers

Understanding that languages change is a critical concept for teachers to grasp. Teachers need to understand this concept so that they can answer questions about language. ELLs often ask why a certain word or grammatical structure is used in novels, but not used in everyday speech or even academic writing. Understanding that there may have been some language changes since the publication of the novel can help in student comprehension and contextualization of the novel. One thing teachers can do is to provide a list of English words that have changed in meaning and then to discuss them with students.

Activities for Teachers

Activity 1: Language Attitudes

Think about the most beautiful prose that you have ever heard. For me it would have to be the final two pages of *A Tale of Two Cities*. I read this Dickens classic my senior year in high school and struggled mightily because it just did not grab me. I doubt if it grabs many seventeen-year-olds. However, I was absolutely enthralled by the last two pages. I found them heroic and beautiful. Now, imagine someone reading that passage aloud in a dialect you did not like. Does this change your perception of the passage and, more important, the person who possesses such an accent? How are your impressions of the text altered by having the passage in different dialects or accents?

Teachers of ELLs should be aware of how dialects and accents affect our perceptions of students. If we work with ELLs, we must be mindful that some will never produce what we imagine to be an "ideal" version of English. Students see our frustrations and consternations about language and dialects, so we must be careful to guard against them.

Activity 2: Language and Standards

Choose ten words or phrases that you hear in common everyday speech that bother you. Some examples might be:

- We're open *24/7*.

- That's *between you and I*.

- It's getting to be *supper* time.

Examine why each bothers you. Is it because it sounds too "hip" *(24/7)*, is it because someone is trying to sound "high-falutin" *(between you and I)*, or is it because it sounds old-fashioned *(supper)* to some people? Try to track down the origins of these words or phrases using dictionaries, grammar books, or other sources. As language teachers we are always aware of language (an occupational hazard), but we also must be willing to analyze our feelings about language change.

Activity 3: Rule of English

It is often claimed that English has more quirks than most languages, but actually all languages have quirks. Nevertheless, teachers should know something about the language. We need to see what is "under the hood." With this in mind, try to explain the following:

- *The lights went off* versus *The alarms went off.*

- *Do you have the time?* versus *Do you have time?*

- *I'll drive over to the store* versus *I'll drive to the store.*

- *The CIA, UCLA, the NSA, MIT, IBM, NASA*

These are some perplexing examples of our English language. How would you explain that *the lights going off* means "off," while *the alarms went off* means that they "came on"? In the second example, intonation means everything. In the first one, *Do you have the time?* can mean two things: "What time is it?" and "Do you have enough time" to do something? The second one only inquires whether someone is busy. In the third example, why is the *over* included? Does it serve a function? Finally, what is the rule about using a determiner with initials and acronyms? When do you use it, and when do you not?

Additional Resources

- The Linguistic Society of America maintains a list of current news articles related to language issues. These are updated regularly and are good places to find articles that relate to current issues. See *www.lsadc.org/info/ling-news.cfm.*

- The 1941 film *Ball of Fire* has a wonderful scene regarding a lexicographer coming to the realization that language cannot be studied apart from the people that use it. He leaves his ivory tower and heads into the world in search of real slang. This may be a fun and helpful way to understand this topic.

- Gene Searchinger's *The Human Language Series* is a three-part documentary from Equinox Films dealing with some of the most fundamental concepts in language. Prominent linguists as well as comedians are interviewed about language.

- The British television series *The Adventure of English* from Films for the Humanities by Melvyn Bragg is an eight-part series on the history of English.

CHAPTER 2

Myths about First Language Acquisition

*There is in every child a painstaking teacher, so skillful that he
obtains identical results in all children in all parts of the world.
The only language men ever speak perfectly is the one they learn
in babyhood, when no one can teach them anything!*

—Maria Montessori, 1949

Parents have an instinctive understanding that language skills are among
the most crucial for a child's success, and indeed they are. Yet parents are
not always quite sure how to develop these language skills. They worry
if they are doing the right things to teach their children language. The
reality is that no one teaches a first language. Try as we might to teach
it, language acquisition just happens. Maria Montessori was not a professional linguist, but her quote perfectly captures a fundamental truth
about learning a first language: Language acquisition happens and is not
taught by parents.

The misconceptions discussed in this chapter are:

1. Parents teach children language, and children learn it through
   imitation.
2. "Parentese" slows language development.
3. Children benefit from having their language corrected.
4. Television aids language development in children.

---

❶ **Misconception:** Parents teach children language, and children learn it through imitation.
Truth: Children are born with an innate ability to acquire language; they do require language input.

Toddlers learn a language from their parents, siblings, and friends without ever being explicitly taught it. If you think about it, how could it be otherwise? If acquiring a first language depended on explicit teaching, then some children would never learn a language. Some cultures really try to teach their children language. But this is not the case for every family or culture. Many cultures do not "teach" language. Regardless of the culture and its attitude toward teaching language, all children do learn language.

Language: An Internal System

All children learn their native language, and they acquire grammatical aspects in a remarkably uniform way. For example, children acquiring English as a native language acquire the progressive verb form *(-ing)* before they acquire the past tense. Similarly, English-speaking children acquire the use of prepositions before they acquire the use of subordinate clauses (Brown, 1973). English-speaking children are not taught progressives or past tenses; they acquire them when they are cognitively ready and after hearing them enough times. They need language input. The input triggers the language system to develop.

Certainly some children seem to acquire language faster than others, but this has more to do with social/cognitive maturation and personality than with the kind of language instruction received. Despite varying levels of speed, children will acquire language in a manner that is uniform and determined largely by biology; we are, as many linguists like to say, "prewired" for language, and the specific language we hear sets the specific parameters for this wiring.

Roger Brown's classic longitudinal study (1973) of "Adam," "Eve," and "Sarah" demonstrates quite clearly that this pre-wiring results in a remarkable consistency in children's emerging speech in terms of the order of acquisition, given normal and interactive input. In this study, Brown visited three toddlers several times a month for one year. He recorded and analyzed their natural speech. His results confirm that the development process is "approximately invariant" for all learners. These data indicate that input activates pre-existing and pre-wired cognitive pathways designed specifically for language. The chart illustrates the order of morpheme acquisition of English learners (Brown, 1973).

Morpheme Acquisition Order for Learners of English as a First Language
ing
-*s* (plural)
irregular past tense
-'*s* (possessive)
copula (linking word)
the, a
-*ed*
-*s* (third singular)
auxiliary *be*

One of the clearest examples of this wiring that allows such rapid and uniform language acquisition is prepositional phrases. Languages have two possible formats for prepositional usage. One format puts the prepositional word before its noun. This is what happens in English and Spanish: *The book is <u>under</u> the table. El libro está <u>debajo de</u> la mesa.* The nouns *table* and *mesa* follow the prepositions *under* and *debajo de*. The other format puts the preposition after the noun that serves as its object. This is the system in Japanese: *hon wa teeburu no shita ni aru/The book is the table <u>under</u>.* In this sentence *shita* means "under," and *teeburu* means "table." Note that *shita* comes after *teeburu*. Since the prepositions come after their nouns, they are called postpositions. Notice that the word *preposition* is derived from pre-position. This example illustrates the binary nature of language parameters in the grammar. We simply set a parameter for our preposition use depending on whether our native language has prepositions or postpositions. As children, after absorbing enough input, we form grammar in our heads. Our wiring allows us to flip the language binary switch much quicker. After we have flipped enough switches, our language grammar system begins to form.

The uniformity in the order of language acquisition is evidence of this innate ability inside a child's brain to learn language just by listening and interacting with native speakers. Linguists call this ability the Language Acquisition Device (L.A.D.). The L.A.D. is a much more efficient system than trying to teach all the grammar of a language. This, of course, cannot be done because there is too much to teach in too little time. Linguist Noam Chomsky called this the *poverty of stimulus theory*.

One famous example (Chomsky, 2004) that illustrates that language is not taught but rather acquired is:

a. John is too stubborn to talk to Bill.

b. John is too stubborn to talk to.

In (a) John will actually do the speaking, but in (b) John is the receiver of a dialogue (or not, depending on his mood). The point is that interpreting these two sentences depends on understanding the structural differences in the sentences. Children beyond a certain age can easily distinguish and interpret them, but they would have a very difficult time explaining the structural differences that result in varied interpretations. It is the categories that reside in a child's mind that allow interpretation. It would be difficult to teach these categories, so the structures are there, ready and waiting for input to stimulate them.

Nature cannot run its course when it comes to language development if circumstances work counter to language acquisition. Parents and teachers can deprive children of language by never interacting with them in meaningful ways. The story of "Genie" is a classic and tragic case of a child being deprived of language. Her story is chronicled in Susan Curtis' *Genie: A Psycholinguistic Study of a Modern Day "Wild Child"* (1977).

Genie was a neglected child who was discovered by a social worker in 1970. Though details are sketchy about what happened to her, it appears that her parents had locked her in a room and fed her, but they never spoke to her. She was discovered when she was thirteen years old, and she was removed from her home. Despite years of rehabilitation and remarkable progress in many areas of development, Genie never learned to speak standard English. In essence, her L.A.D. shut down due to lack of stimulation. This is most obvious in the way her use of syntax was affected. She could not use the passive, could not form questions, and had trouble with pronouns. She did make some progress in language but could not form a complete English grammar (Curtis, 1977).

Fortunately, cases such as Genie's are rare, but they underscore the importance of interaction to achieve language acquisition, and they encourage parents to interact with their young children by speaking, pointing, naming, cooing, and smiling. A reasonably interactive environment appears to be sufficient for language acquisition to take place and such a situation does not require explicit teaching, just basic interaction.

An equally sad case is "Michael." Michael was a young child when his Italian immigrant parents came to the United States. Michael's parents were determined to have him learn English so they refused to use Italian in their home. The problem was that the parents did not know English, so Michael grew up with little language input at a time in his life when such input is critical. In essence, Michael was stuck in a linguistic no man's land because he was not receiving the input necessary in English nor Italian to trigger the innate language structures in his brain (Piper, 1998).

Cases such as Genie's and Michael's have serious implications for the ELL. These learners should <u>not</u> be encouraged to abandon their native language particularly at a young age. Such a strategy, as David Crystal points out, can easily result in "a bilingual ... never achieving native-like fluency in either" (Crystal, 2007, p. 412). Michael did eventually learn English, but very slowly since school-English was insufficient to learn all that he needed. It is not important which language a child develops; the important thing is that the child develops a language. This is done not by explicit teaching, but by exposure to and interaction with a language. This interaction and the child's L.A.D. will allow the child to develop a language (Brown, 2007).

Parents may teach some aspects of language like the lexicon, but most of the lexicon (and the rest of the language system) develops by itself. As Stephen Pinker (1994), an MIT psychologist, notes, children are "lexical vacuum cleaners" because from eighteen months to three years of age, they learn about ten words a day. Parents cannot teach this many, and they do not have to. The fact is, no one misses out on language acquisition if there is exposure to and interaction with language and no serious physical or cognitive impairment.

Children need exposure to and interaction with language, and parents' natural instinct for reading, singing, and playing language games with their babies and toddlers is a most useful and beneficial instinct. But children acquire the parts of language that are natural for them at a given point in their cognitive development and not necessarily when we think they should be ready to learn specific aspects of the language. For instance, while we may be reading a story about colors, the child, in fact, may not be processing the names of colors but the sounds of the language. The child may be processing the placement of prepositions in sentences. There is simply no way to know what is being processed at a given moment; thus the futility of trying to "teach" a first language.

Along with teaching a first language, many people believe in the erroneous notion that language acquisition occurs as a result of imitation. The explanation of language acquisition by imitation has a very intuitive appeal: children learn language by imitating their parents. It is a seemingly logical explanation that seems to settle the question of child language acquisition. Yet, when examined closely, this reasoning falls short. Although I have argued against imitation as the reason for first language acquisition in my linguistics class, students who hold this theory are not willing to give up the imitation explanation even in the face of evidence. The two arguments against imitation, while simple, are irrefutable.

• *Argument 1. Originality in sentences.* Children say all sorts of things that they have never heard. How would this be possible if language acquisition occurred exclusively or even primarily through imitation? Waiting to hear every sentence that one would want to say and then memorizing would be a rather inefficient system.

Consider these gems spoken by children:

"I want Pepsi on my cereal."

"I love Barney."

"Can I eat butter?"

With the exception of a few adults with very undiscerning tastes who may have uttered these sentences, children create such sentences all by themselves. In other words, they create new sentences and do not imitate anyone. Children can and do memorize some phrases, which gives the illusion that imitation is key to language acquisition. Children memorize phrases like, *Can I take a message?* or *You look nice.* These are small polite phrases that seem to work for adults, so naturally, a child uses them. Despite these few imitated phrases, the overwhelming majority (indeed almost all) of a child's utterances are unique and could not possibly have been memorized.

• *Argument 2. Child-created errors.* Children say ill-formed sentences. When a child articulates sentences such as *They laugh me* for *They tickle me,* they demonstrate an ability to create sentences that they have never heard.

A toddler also uses phrases like *Let go me.* My youngest daughter often says this when it is time to take some rather awful-tasting medicine. Her intent is to run away and play to avoid the ill-tasting concoction. I understand her utterance perfectly and her distaste for liquid medicine, but no one has ever said this exact phrase to her. She takes the bits of grammar she knows and forms this sentence, breaking one rule in English grammar that requires the direct object to come before the verb in this kind of construction. She could not possibly be imitating anyone because she has never heard this sort of construction in English. Children also regularize irregular endings. They create these utterances despite never having heard them.

A Child's Regularization of Irregular Forms in English
went → goed
children → childs
better → gooder
brought → bringed
(Fromkin, Rodman, & Hyams, 2006)

If we listen to adult conversations, we notice something else. We all stop, stutter, repeat, start over, and put in the wrong word during conversations. Children do not imitate somebody's conversational stumbles; they commit their own.

This debate between imitation and grammar construction in language acquisition was actually the spark for much of modern linguistics. In 1957 the behaviorist psychologist B. F. Skinner published a book entitled *Verbal Behavior* in which he argued that language is stimulus controlled, and thus imitation of correct patterns (and positive reinforcement for them) is key to learning language. Noam Chomsky (1959) refuted this argument in his review of the book by demonstrating that an L.A.D. device already exists and that it is the main element in language development. Today, most linguists side with Chomsky, but it seems that the general public agrees with Skinner's position and, in fact, Skinner had been required reading in teacher education programs for decades. Fifty years later, the debate continues, and Skinner's position continues to find support.

Implications for Teachers

Teachers need not be overly concerned with grammatical accuracy, particularly at a young age and at the earliest stages of English acquisition. Providing a language acquisition-rich environment has a lasting language effect on the child. A language-rich environment is one in which teachers define words, expose students to different kinds of English, and encourage creativity with the language. Teachers should be more concerned with this (both for native and ELLs) in their classrooms.

---

❷ **Misconception:** "Parentese" slows language development.
Truth: "Parentese" acts as a tutorial for young language learners.

If babies and toddlers use their L.A.D.s to construct grammars based on the input they receive, it seems logical to assume that the input should be high quality and not infantile. In other words, input should be free of parentese (the simplified form of language that parents use with babies and toddlers, also called motherese). Parents are often told to avoid parentese because the fear associated with its use is that the child will not develop mature speaking patterns. On the June 7, 2004 broadcast of the *Dr. Phil Show*, Dr. Phil admonished parents to not say *wawa* if their toddler wanted water. Dr. Phil was of the opinion that "baby-talk" was detrimental to a child's language development. As he said, "You don't want your seventh grader asking his gym teacher for *wawa*." Dr. Phil's advice was to train children to speak *correctly* from the beginning and, apparently, this sort of baby talk was, in his opinion, not conducive to developing mature speaking patterns. Some mothers insist that no parentese be used with their child because they mistakenly think that the child will speak correctly only if everyone speaks like adults to the child. According to Dougherty (2000), "Experts believe that you should not use or encourage baby talk."

An Analysis of Baby Talk

So what does baby talk consist of? Universal aspects of baby talk involve word reduction (some sounds are eliminated such as *pacy* for *pacifier*), word repetition *(night night),* sentence simplification, and the use of a higher pitch.

Toddlers cannot produce as many sounds as adults, but they can distinguish more sounds. In fact, babies can easily distinguish sounds in any human language. However, over time they slowly lose this ability, and they begin to focus on the sounds of the language or languages that they hear most often. Apparently, baby talk helps them focus on the sounds of their language.

The syntax in English is also important, and it takes time to acquire the subtleties of using it. For instance, children do not begin to understand the passive voice *(The ball was kicked by the child)* until they are four or five years old. Parents instinctively seem to avoid this sentence pattern until about that age. Parents can use passive construction when the child is two or three, but it will be beyond the child's comprehension.

So how does baby talk help language development? Languages of the world have space between vowels. For instance, the vowels /i/, /a/, and, /u/ are pronounced by moving the tongue to different regions of the mouth. For a word like *beat,* the tongue comes all the way forward; for a word like *lot,* the tongue drops low; and for a word like *boot,* the tongue moves to the back of the mouth. These are the outside limits of all vowel sounds that the human vocal tract can produce. Motherese accentuates the vowels by emphasizing them and elongating them. Research (Kuhl, 2004) shows that this vowel elongation is done by mothers speaking languages as diverse as English, Russian, and Swedish.

What all this indicates is that baby talk becomes a tutorial and helps babies focus on the sounds and grammar of their language (Kuhl, 2004). Word reduction and simplification help lexical development. Vowel elongation helps the child identify the vowels in later conversations. The elimination of grammar features (such as passives) helps children organize syntactic rules and delays complicated grammar until they are ready. And the higher pitch can keep their attention. Interestingly, as the toddler becomes developmentally ready for more complicated grammatical structures, baby talk by parents diminishes. Baby talk is not harmful, but rather quite natural and beneficial because it makes the baby focus on language. So parents should not be hesitant to use parentese.

- The phenomenon of speaking parentese is quite universal. Patricia Kuhl, a neuroscientist at the University of Washington, led a team of researchers studying baby talk around the world. They discovered that baby talk follows a similar pattern regardless of language and helps babies discover and unravel their language (Kuhl, 2004, p. 839). While a few cultures do not use it (Charles Yang offers evidence that Kaluli speakers in Papau New Guinea do not alter speech for children [2006, p. 90]), most cultures do employ baby talk, especially when they are at home alone with their child and there are no researchers around. So almost everyone does it, but mainstream thinking maintains that it is wrong. Linguists, however, assure us that it is not wrong.

When the British television children's program *Teletubbies* (a live action show featuring four make-believe characters) began airing in the United States, there was much concern because the characters used toddler-talk (Freeman, 1998). Parents complained about their toddlers being exposed to "toddlerese." The producers responded to complaints by toning down the toddler-talk and by giving the characters an American accent when they spoke toddlerese.

Implications for Teachers

While teachers are understandably not thinking about using parentese in a classroom, there is a valuable lesson to be taken from this research. Teachers' pedagogical approaches should be informed by the fact that simplified speech (a slower rate, repeating, and defining terms) for ELLs is a very effective method of delivering instruction. This type of speech also allows ELLs to understand the content better, and it assists them in developing a new grammar not unlike they did when they developed their first language grammar. This is *not* considered baby talk.

> ❸ **Misconception:** Children benefit from having their language corrected.
>
> **Truth:** Correcting a child's language has limited benefits.

Ask most parents, and they will say that they believe correction is necessary for language development. However, research has shown that parents only correct a very small portion of their child's language, and a large percentage of these are "dirty words."

Recently my wife and daughter picked me up from work. When I got in the car, my four-year-old daughter asked me if I was wearing my new watch. I told her that I did not have a new watch. She replied, "Oh, yes, you do. Mommy and me just *buyed* it for you before we picked you up. We're going to give it to you for your birthday." Now, there are those who would claim that my daughter should have been corrected: "*Bought, not buyed.*" But my wife, laughingly, corrected her for spoiling the surprise instead. We never corrected her whenever she said *buyed,* and now she says *bought.* Similarly, when my youngest daughter says things like, *Me do that* or *I no like it,* she is usually smiled at and rarely corrected.

Although language correction does no harm, it has very little effect. Children will correct themselves over time to conform to standard speech patterns if they are exposed to them. Eventually irregular verbs like *bought* are added to a child's language skills, not because of correction, but because of exposure.

The distinctive linguistic pattern of this irregular verb is that children start out saying *bought* because that is what they hear. Children *imitate* this for a while, but then they switch to *buyed* once they figure out English's *-ed* rule to form past tense and then they overapply it to words like *buyed* and *teached.* When they switch to *bought* in their mature speech patterns, it is because they recognize it as an irregular form that defied the *-ed* rule.

There are some things that can and should be "corrected" at home or at school if we want to develop fluency in the standard dialect for mainstream and ELL students. For instance, the past participle of *to bring* is *brought.* However, many speakers of various dialects in the United

States use *brung*. Once children are older and have started school, they are cognitively ready to handle this sort of correction. Teachers who are familiar with standard American English will be able to point out the non-standard usage such as *brung*, but when students are surrounded by a non-standard form such as *brung* in the home and in the community, it might be difficult for students to use this spontaneously as they will often revert to the form they hear most often. This affords teachers the opportunity to discuss issues such as formal and informal language and when each is appropriate. Similarly, ELLs will be exposed to both standard and non-standard forms, and this will have to be explained. The issue of correction for ELLs is more complicated and will be discussed in Chapter 3.

Correction has always been an issue in language. On an episode of *I Love Lucy* that aired in 1952, Lucy decides to hire an English tutor to correct her English and the English of her husband and neighbors because she wants her baby to grow up hearing only "correct" English. Of course, the whole affair is a fiasco. The English tutor refuses to allow his pupils to say words like *okay* and *swell*. It is all rather humorous, but it is problematic to use the word *correct* even when we teach children.

It is futile to try to eliminate the use of *okay* and *swell* by correcting speech. And what about pronunciation? Should we correct speakers of southern English when they pronounce *genuine* with *wine* on the end. By standards in the rest of the country, the southern pronunciation of this word is marked (a term used in linguistics to denote non-standard) but it isn't for speakers of the southern U.S. dialect. What about *mischievous*? I have heard people pronounce it with a long /i/ in the middle, but language purists would correct this. The point is this: It is very difficult to determine "correct" pronunciation because every region has its own unique way of pronouncing English. The English in New Jersey is vastly different from the English in south Texas and even different still from the English in India and Nigeria (where there are, in fact, many native speakers of English). But difference is not better or worse, or more or less correct. Just different.

Implications for Teachers

ELLs, like first language learners, may not benefit that much from correction. In fact, ELLs have other issues that may prevent them from learning from correction. If correction causes them a great deal of embarrassment in class, productive learning will not occur. In addition, research shows that correction is limited in its effectiveness because while teachers may correct, there may be limited **uptake** (internalization of the correction that alters a grammatical system) (Brown, 2007). Here is an example of a typical ELL error and correction pattern. A rule of English states that on regular third-person verbs, an -s is added (e.g., *walks, lives*). However, this rule is late acquired in the ELLs' English acquisition process. Though it may be corrected many times, an ELL may forget to use it in spontaneous speech. Teachers should not get frustrated by this, and they should not frustrate students with overcorrection. Brown (2007, pp. 277–279) offers some advice to assist teachers as they determine whether they should correct errors. At times correction may be helpful, but teachers should consider these factors:

- purpose of the classroom activity (brainstorming versus editing a piece of writing)
- the student's ability to handle correction (linguistically and emotionally)
- severity of the error (a small local error such as a wrong verb ending or a larger global error such as using a wrong word)
- source of the error (slip of the tongue versus a systematic pattern)

Teachers should evaluate these elements and then decide which elements should be judiciously corrected.

> ❹ **Misconception:** Television aids language development in children.
> **Truth:** TV may enhance vocabulary in older children, but TV does not promote language development.

More than a decade ago, a popular video series for children called *Baby Einstein* was developed specifically for babies and toddlers. It features visual images, sounds, rhymes, stories, and music for the infant and toddler to watch. The producers claimed that watching the videos helps children in their cognitive and language development. Controversy has surrounded this claim by this and similar video series. The American Academy of Pediatrics recommends that children under two should watch little or no television. It makes this recommendation in response to research that indicates one- to two-year-olds in the United States average three to four hours of TV daily (Andrews, 2002). This much TV cannot be wonderful for young children and may actually be harmful to the development of eyesight, may cause over-stimulation, and may lead to shorter attention spans. Yet parents may convince themselves that TV and video series like *Baby Einstein*, while not perfect, have significant benefits for language development. On the surface television seems to provide good language input, and it can appear that the child is engaged with it. But in reality, the child is not really engaged with the language on TV. Dimitri Christakis and a team of researchers at the University of Washington recently released a study that says that TV can even be detrimental to language development by limiting time with real language interaction (Schmidt, 2006).

In 2003, Robin Close was commissioned by the National Literacy Trust to review the research on television and language development. Her review was published as "Television and language development in the early years: A review of the literature" in 2004 by the National Literacy Trust in London. She has concluded that language development depends more on interaction and that television cannot produce the interaction needed. The research shows some benefits from television but only for older children and that limiting all television for children under two years of age seems prudent. Older children (age 3+) can learn some vocabulary from television and perhaps some concepts, but early language development does not garner enough benefit from television to support the evident overuse of television with infants and toddlers. It is the interaction with caregivers that prompts true language development. In fairness to *Baby Einstein*'s producers, they recommend caregivers watch with the baby and talk with them about what is on the screen.

Television has a very small positive staying power when it comes to language development. *Baby Einstein* has no damaging effect unless toddlers watch too much TV, then they are missing out on real language development with parents, siblings, and friends.

Implications for Teachers

Teachers, like parents, need to provide language-rich environments, and this entails meaningful interaction with oral language. TV and computers may be tools in giving some assistance, but they are poor substitutes for real language interaction.

Activities for Teachers

Activity 1: Toddler Speech

Ask three friends who have children if they correct their toddlers' speech. If they do claim to correct it, find out what elements they correct: pronunciation, verb tenses, syntax. Then try to find instances of when this occurs. Ask if they use baby talk with their infant or toddler. Do they seem apologetic if they do?

Activity 2: Language Quotations

Do a search on the Internet for "Language Quotations." There are several sites that will provide lists of quotations. Find three quotes about learning a first language that you agree with and three that you disagree with. Explain why.

Activity 3: Group Work

There is debate among ELL teachers regarding whether their students' English language development will be impeded if they listen to other ELLs' "bad English." Some teachers avoid group work so this will not happen. Is this a sound pedagogical strategy? This relates to the discussion of baby talk and first language acquisition. Find two articles (or two ELL teachers) with opposite views of this. What are the main points on each side?

Additional Resources

- The video *A Child's Guide to Language* (Films for the Humanities, Inc., 1983) provides interesting discussion points as it compares first and second language acquisition. Though somewhat dated, it is an interesting exploration of the topic.

- The PBS series *The Secret Life of the Brain* (2002) dedicates its second episode to language. In *The Child's Brain: From Syllable to Sound,* many issues about learning a first language are discussed (phoneme recognition, age, and acquisition) as well as what can go wrong so that a child may not develop a language.

- The PBS documentary *Secret of the Wild Child* (1994) is a fascinating and disturbing video about the life and care of Genie after she was discovered. Through interviews with the specialists who worked with Genie, the video explores the linguistic and ethical implications of her case.

CHAPTER **3**

Myths about Second Language Acquisition

Americans who travel abroad for the first time are often shocked to discover that, despite all the progress that has been made in the last 30 years, many foreign people still speak in foreign languages.

—Dave Barry, 1988

Few Americans are proficient in a second language, yet they seem to criticize ELLs for not learning English quickly. This criticism is not only ironic, it also demonstrates a plethora of misunderstandings about second language acquisition. This chapter will clarify some of these misconceptions and show how policies or viewpoints based on these misconceptions do a disservice to ELLs. The misconceptions discussed in this chapter are:

1. Recent immigrants to the United States learn English more slowly than previous generations of immigrants.
2. Young L2 learners should be completely immersed in English.
3. Smart people are better second language learners.
4. Grammar has no place in second language instruction.
5. Listening and reading are the easiest skills to acquire in a second language.

> **❶ Misconception:** Recent immigrants to the United States learn English more slowly than previous generations of immigrants.
>
> **Truth:** Today's immigrants are learning English as a second language at the same rate as previous generations of immigrants.

The complaint that recent immigrants are not learning English quickly enough is common. As Guadalupe Valdes, an ESL researcher, notes, "In the current context in which anti-immigrant sentiment is strong, newly arrived children are routinely accused by the general public of not wanting to learn English and of failing to profit from the education that the state is giving to them at great costs" (2001, p. 12). Survey research from 2006 conducted by the Pew Research Center for the People and the Press shows that 58 percent of Americans think that today's immigrants are learning English too slowly. A sampling of editorial pages and posting on blogs indicates this prevailing national sentiment that immigrants and many Americans believe immigrants are even *refusing* to learn:

> Culturally we have shifted from an integrating, English-speaking American citizenship focused model of immigration to an acceptance of foreign habits (which are going to include corruption), foreign loyalties (illustrated by the waving of foreign flags by many of the marchers, some with attitudes of contempt) and the insistence (not necessarily by immigrants) on creating non–English speaking legal and educational structures.
>
> —Gingrich, *National Review Online*, 2006

Those who hold views like these often criticize recent immigrants because they believe that they are lazy or stubborn when it comes to learning English. This attitude affects teachers and school systems because some members of the public will object to ESL teaching programs; they feel ESL programs (for adults and children) are "coddling" the immigrants and diverting educational resources away from native English-speaking students. However, Lucy Tse (2001) documents in her book *Why Don't They Learn English? Separating Fact from Fallacy in the U.S. Language Debate* that the reality is that immigrants today are learning English at the same rate as previous generations of immigrants and that sound ESL programs and strategies help the language acquisition process and do not diminish resources for other students. The assumption that past generations learned quickly is just that, an assumption. If previous generations of immigrants learned English so quickly, why did ethnic enclaves (Chinatown, Germantown) spring into existence? They came into existence at least in part due to the difficulty of learning English and the availability of a comfort zone in their own language enclave. Research like Tse's demonstrates that, contrary to popular opinion, immigrants are learning English as quickly today and that by providing ESL services, school systems assist in the language acquisition process.

Part of the reason for the false perception that immigrants today are taking longer to learn English is due to the three generation rule. When immigrants arrive in the country, the adults (first generation) rarely learn the language with native-like proficiency, although there may be exceptions. The children of these immigrants, second generation, are bilingual in the language of their parents and that of their new country. The third generation is typically monolingual in the language of the country. The case of Spanish-speaking immigrants illustrates the public's seeming frustration with immigrants and the acquisition of English. The pattern is as stable today as in the past, but the sustained influx of Spanish-speaking immigrants is responsible for giving the perception of a "refusal" to learn English, while in fact it is simply new immigrants. The percentage of foreign-born Hispanics has dramatically risen since 1980: According to Ramirez (2004, p. 9), 46 percent of foreign-born Hispanic residents entered the United States between 1990 and 2000, compared to 29 percent of foreign-born Hispanic residents who entered the United States between 1980 and 1990. The Census Bureau also reports that in 2000, more than 40 percent of all Hispanic residents are foreign born. This sort of sustained immigration provides a continual influx of native–Spanish speakers in the United States. However, like previous immigrants, Hispanics place a high priority on learning English. Surveys show that 85 percent of immigrants place a high value on learning English and recognize the difficulty of getting a job without English (Farkas, 2003).

Many Americans simply forget how difficult it is or how long it takes to learn a second language, thus the perceptions that immigrants should do it more quickly. If more Americans became fluent in an L2 or at least attempted to do so, they would appreciate the struggle and the years of dedication it takes to master an L2, and they would be less likely to attribute ELLs' failure and slow progress to laziness and stubbornness. Americans are not necessarily being belligerent; they simply do not understand. I always tell students in my TESOL methods courses that there is a very cyclical nature to the demand that immigrants learn English and the complaint that they are not doing so quickly enough. Cavanaugh (1996) traces the history of English teaching from colonial times to the present day and notes that many policies were instituted out of frustration that current immigrants were not learning English quickly enough. For example, after the Revolutionary War, there were laments that immigrants were not learning quickly enough. Cavanaugh's conclusions are that this frustration precedes periods when there is a strong national push for English classes, and indeed since the earliest educational systems in the United States, there have been ESL classes for non-native speakers. Many times these classes are offered for altruistic reasons, such as helping immigrants find work, and sometimes the classes are offered for more hegemonic and xenophobic motives (Cavanaugh, 1996). In essence, Cavanaugh concludes, there have always been ESL classes, but they have not always been the best sort of classes for quickly acquiring English.

Implications for Teachers

Even with very good ESL classes, research by Cummins (1996) estimates that it takes an ESL student five to seven years to reach a proficiency level in English so that he or she could do grade-level academic work. Collier and Thomas (1997) estimate that it might actually take an ESL student up to ten years to attain this level of proficiency if he or she has had little or no education in the primary language. Collier and Thomas conclude based on this data that English-only classrooms are inefficient for low proficiency–level ESL students with little education and that bilingual education programs are much more suited to help these students attain a high level of academic English. Teachers' roles as advocates for ELL call them to dispel the myth that ELLs are not learning English quickly. They could also advocate for more dual-language education systems in the United States. There are great possibilities for a dual-language education system in the United States that would produce more bilingual students (Lindholm-Leary, 2001). Such a system would focus on helping immigrants learn English and helping English-speaking students learn an L2 (perhaps Spanish, because this language is the largest language minority in the United States) and perhaps "eradicate the negative status of bilingualism in the United States (Lindholm-Leary, p. 1). Many countries (Canada, India, Kenya) have dual-language education systems, and they function well. Such a system in the United States could work if political discussions were left out and there was instead more emphasis on second language learning.

❷ **Misconception:** Young L2 learners should be completely immersed in English.
Truth: Young learners benefit from development in their first language.

Many people think that since ELL children learn a second language more quickly, more easily, and better than adults, they should be completely and quickly immersed in English. The quotes below from popular media perpetuate the false notion that children learn all aspects of a new language more quickly than adults and with less effort.

☼ Media Spotlight

From both a practical teaching standpoint as well as the latest research, we now know that the better learner is one who starts early—as least before 10.

(Holman, *Better Homes and Gardens*, 1988)

Children up to the age of puberty learn languages much more easily.

(Winslow, *Wall Street Journal*, 1997)

Not only is learning a foreign language easier for children than it is for adults, but children who are exposed to other languages also do better in school, score higher on standardized tests, are better problem solvers and are more open to diversity.

(Walton, 2007)

Scientific conjecture based on research in first language acquisition research seems to support the idea that learning a second language is most efficient when the learner is young. Eric Lenneberg, a psychologist, published an article in 1964 that suggested that there is a limited window of opportunity for children to learn a first language. This phenomenon is known as the critical-age hypothesis. If a child does not acquire a language during this period, Lennenberg postulated, it will be impossible for him or her to do so. This critical age *appears* to explain why young children learn a *second* language with relative ease and adults struggle: The children are in the critical period and are able to grasp the second language. There is just one problem: Children do *not* necessarily learn faster, more easily, or attain higher levels of proficiency in all areas of a second language (Modern Language Association, 2006). While there are studies (Johnson & Newport, 1989; Patkowski, 1980) that indicate age is a factor in second language acquisition (SLA), there are no studies that conclude definitively that children outperform adults in all areas of SLA.

Despite inconclusive evidence that children have a magical ability for learning an L2, many teachers and administrators advocate that ELLs be completely immersed in English. Immersion, they believe, will ensure that children tap into this ability that diminishes with age, and thus they will be fluent in English quickly and with little effort. However, this immersion strategy can have detrimental effects on first and second language development. Chapter 2 discussed the case of Michael, who was denied access to Italian, his native language. The result was poor language development in both English and Italian. Development in one language has effects on all subsequent languages learned. We should encourage continued development of the L1 of young ELLs because it will ultimately help with proficiency in English. It also allows children to avoid feeling "invisible," which is how Norma Mota-Altman (2003), a bilingual teacher, described her experience in an English immersion program. Since she did not know English, she felt that no one "believed she could do anything or say anything of value" at school.

Bilingual education programs, which teach content in the native language of the students while the students also learn English, allow the children to feel less invisible because their native language is used at least part of the school day. However, such programs are often criticized on political and economic grounds. For example, voters in California passed Proposition 227 in 1998, which outlawed bilingual education programs that they felt were too expensive and did not demonstrate effectiveness. However, the best possible course of action for young ELLs is for the school system to support the continued growth and development of the students' native language while they are learning English. However, limited funding and political pressure makes the future of bilingual education programs tenuous in many communities (Cavanaugh, 1996).

One area of SLA in which young learners do indeed excel is pronunciation. If exposed to a second language, young children develop a more native-like pronunciation than their adult counterparts (McLaughlin, 1992). There are neural and physiological reasons for this, but the young children (after toddlerhood) do not have a distinctive advantage over adults in other areas of language development. In the other areas of language learning such as grammatical accuracy and lexical retention, children do not hold an advantage, so complete immersion is not always the best approach for all ELLs.

Implications for Teachers

There is one piece of detrimental advice parents sometimes receive from teachers on the issue of bilingualism that, if followed, could impair language development. Teachers and school administrators sometimes instruct immigrant parents to use *only* English in the home. Diane Materazzi, a bilingual specialist in California, said, "Teachers used to tell parents to only speak English at home. That was straining the bonds between parents and their children" (Frank, 1993). It also does not improve English proficiency. Teachers give this advice to facilitate the rapid acquisition of English by the child. It *seems* logical and intuitive, but this advice is based on an incomplete understanding of the language acquisition process.

For a young child between four and six years of age, the language acquisition process is not complete. It is absolutely critical that a child fully develop a language. This allows the child to perform all sorts of complicated cognitive functions: exploring, interacting, naming, and listening. If the child's parents are not fully proficient speakers of English and they try to switch to only their limited English, then in essence, the child would get an incomplete picture of both languages and neither language would be fully acquired. Some researchers in linguistics have labeled this subtractive bilingualism (the introduction of a second language in a manner that inhibits development in the first) (Lightbown & Spada, 1999). This means that, especially for elementary school students, it is essential that teachers and parents encourage the home language to develop fully rather than stunt its growth by attempting to force a second language in which the child does not get adequate input.

I often wonder how many times French-speaking parents are told by teachers to stop speaking French to their children. I suspect, due to the prestige of French in the United States compared to other languages, native French speakers are encouraged to use French in the home with their children, while others are told to use only English. In this situation, a teacher's feelings about a language supersede linguistic reality.

❸ **Misconception:** Smart people are better second language learners.
Truth: Intelligence and L2 learning are not correlated.

In our society we tend to think that polyglots (individuals fluent in several languages) are really smart people. Cardinal Guiseppe Mezzofanti (1774–1849), once a librarian at the Vatican, reportedly knew how to speak 50 languages and could translate 114 (Crystal, 2007, p. 416). Most people would say this was a clear sign of intelligence. Cardinal Mezzofanti no doubt was highly intelligent; however, are we to infer then that foreign languages are only for smart people? Should we assume that only really smart ELLs will learn English with a high degree of proficiency? The answer to both is no. In fact, intelligence correlates very poorly with L2 acquisition. There are other factors that correlate higher with success in an L2: motivation, tolerance for ambiguity, and self-esteem (Brown, 2007).

To explain this misconception, intelligence must be defined. I am using the term here as a traditional notion of intelligence quotient or IQ. It is a measure of "one's linguistic and logical-mathematical abilities" (Brown,

2007, p. 108). For the purpose of this discussion, this is how the notion of intelligence will be used here.

People often brag that they know two or three languages as if this is an indication of their intelligence. Academics, including linguists, are often the worst in encouraging the supposition that knowledge of two or more languages reveals their intelligence. They love to flaunt their language prowess by throwing out a few words in their many languages. But what is in actuality the true relationship between intelligence and second language learning?

A Case Study of Intelligence and Second Languages

One of the most remarkable examples of how traditional notions of IQ and language learning ability are not in a one-to-one relationship is the case of "Christopher," a language savant. Christopher has a severely limited IQ (around 50) and cannot play a game as simple as checkers because he cannot grasp the rules. However, with virtually no formal instruction, Christopher can communicate in sixteen languages (Danish, Dutch, Finnish, French, German, Greek, Hindi, Italian, Norwegian, Polish, Portuguese, Russian, Spanish, Swedish, Turkish, and Welsh) with varying degrees of proficiency (Fromkin, Rodman, & Hyams, 2006). This by itself is evidence that language and general intelligence have no direct correlation. In fact, they appear to be very independent systems, despite the fact that we use language to express and even formulate our thinking.

Intelligence is not a prerequisite for proficiency in a second language, although people with high IQs do pass traditional grammar tests with high scores—but this does not constitute "knowing" the language. Robert Gardner and Wallace Lambert (1972) pioneered work in attitudes and motivation in second language learning. Their work clearly demonstrates that attitude and motivation correlate higher with successful L2 learning than intelligence. The fact is, average students often fare better in language acquisition because they do not overanalyze. They simply speak. High-achieving students, on the other hand, often seem to worry and wait until everything is perfect before they speak, thus restricting their own language development. And yet, many schools, teachers, and parents seem convinced that only the smart kids can learn a second language. In 1923, a New York public school superintendent recommended that "slower students" should be given more periods of study during the school day and be spared from foreign language because it is too difficult. What the superintendent said is echoed today when college-bound students are encouraged to take a second language in high school, while other students are not.

Implications for Teachers

ELLs who struggle with English are sometimes viewed as less intelligent than other ELLs who excel in language learning. What teachers and school systems must realize is that ELLs who struggle with English may not have any cognitive deficiencies. In fact, they may be very bright students who have another personality characteristic (e.g., low tolerance for ambiguity) that makes them poor language learners.

A mathematics colleague told me that although she is very talented in mathematics, she was always placed in the lowest level math class in high school because she was an ELL and struggled with English. It was assumed that because of her poor language learning skills, she was not intelligent. Unfortunately, her story is all too common.

There are, of course, instances when an ELL has some learning disability. The ELL population has the same percentage of learning disabled students as the mainstream population. However, ELLs are referred to special education at a disproportionate rate due to their language skills (Echevarria, Vogt, & Short, 2004). Schools must strive to determine which ELLs have disabilities and which are having language problems. They are not the same. If possible, schools should test students with suspected learning disabilities in their native language to determine if special services are required.

> ❹ **Misconception:** Grammar has no place in second language
> instruction. ↦ prudently.
> **Truth:** If used judiciously, explicit grammar instruction aids
> in L2 acquisition. ↳ clear

When it comes to the role of explicit grammar instruction in L2 teaching, there are two extremes: relying exclusively on grammar instruction and omitting grammar all together. Both are detrimental to L2 learning. Some language teaching companies go to the extreme of omitting grammar. *Rosetta Stone*® is a top-selling product for individuals learning an L2 outside of a school setting. The program is available for more than 30 different languages and comes complete with video clips, computer software, and exercises. In its advertisements, *Rosetta Stone*® claims to offer great language skills and cultural awareness, and the company contends that the learning will be effortless, enjoyable, and without grammar. Advocates of the program say such a program helped or gave them a boost in their language learning, but the companies promise so much more.

Is this false advertising? Not exactly. However, this natural ease that they display on many of their advertisements is something they cannot deliver. If some neural pathways for language are compromised through the natural maturation process and if adolescents and adults are more sensitive to linguistic blunders and thus more inhibited, how can second language learning ever happen just like a first language learning? Language companies cannot promise that, but note they do not specify that the end result will be native-like proficiency.

Learning an L2 is hard work. Unless you have constant exposure to the language and are freed of inhibitions, you will struggle. You will need to work to learn the vocabulary and the grammar. But *Rosetta Stone*® suggests hard work with grammar and memorization are unnecessary for L2 acquisition. The company uses the words "naturally and easily" and implies that explicit grammar instruction and memorization are unnecessary.

The role of grammar is a rather contentious issue for teachers with ELLs. Stephen Krashen's (Krashen & Terrel, 1983) notion of comprehensible input (the theory that language is acquired only when learners are exposed to understandable messages and not by grammar instruction) is very important. However, Krashen maintains that teaching grammar is ineffectual and potentially detrimental in all cases, and this position has prompted some teachers to omit explicit grammar instruction entirely. Other researchers (Rutherford, 1987; Ellis, 1994) believe that Krashen's position can be criticized and that there is some interface between explicitly learned grammar in an L2 and the structures that are picked up through exposure. In other words, explicit grammar lessons can help.

The question for teachers is this: How much grammar should be taught? Rutherford's balanced approach makes the most sense because it recognizes that explicit grammar teaching helps, but it is not the only or most critical ingredient for L2 acquisition success. Grammar has an important role to play, but an "overzealous comparison of learning a first language and a second language acquisition" (Folse, 2004, p. vi) has called the role of grammar into question and some mistakenly eliminate grammar.

Some instructors of ELLs reject grammar teaching and succumb to those myths that come from the second language teaching establishment and that are further embellished by the ads such as those for *Rosetta Stone*®. Krashen's ideas about omitting direct grammar instruction are all the more appealing, especially in light of some of our own second language learning experiences. It seems that many people who studied a foreign language can recall a class that was centered, sometimes exclusively, on grammar. Usually by the end of such a class, some students could conjugate verbs, but they could not communicate. Other students, of course, could do neither. Teachers who reflect on their own experience will concur with the conclusions in a 2007 report,

"Foreign Languages and Higher Education: New Structures for a Changed World," produced by a committee from the Modern Language Association. The committee criticized typical foreign language programs "that are characterized by two or three years of grammar and vocabulary taught pretty much in a vacuum, followed by more advanced courses in literature" (Bollag, 2007). Because of this outdated system, teachers have felt liberated by Krashen's endorsement to move away from grammar in classes to more natural approaches, but grammar has its usefulness.

How much grammar instruction in the second language classroom is appropriate and beneficial is a very complicated question. Teachers and students rarely see eye to eye on this. Both have an intuitive sense of what they think is the right amount of grammar. There is a place and a need for both immersion-type instruction and grammar instruction. The key is finding the right combination and then executing it well enough to convince students to trust us and work with us to improve their learning of a second language. If done in moderation and in age-appropriate ways, grammar can be a helpful tool in the acquisition of a second language. Formally learned grammar does help with language learning, and memorization can help key linguistic elements stick with us. However, grammar can be overdone.

Guadalupe Valdes' book, *Learning and Not Learning English* (2001), is an account of the tragic school experiences of four ELLs. The ELLs are in ESL classrooms and fall victim to grammar-based instruction and isolation from natural English input. They are in the "ESL ghetto" as Valdes says, and they cannot escape to the real English world. We know that students benefit from contact with English, yet we have a hard time figuring out how to expose immigrant students (particularly older students) to real English and, at the same time, give them the content needed to keep up with their academic courses. However, if students spend all their time in ESL classes in which only grammar exercises are done and then retreat into their native language after school, it will take a long time indeed for them to attain the necessary proficiency for academic success.

Implications for Teachers

When an ELL has difficulty with an area of English, teachers must decide how best to help him or her. Sometimes a mini-lesson in grammar will help. Other times the grammar explanation will be too complicated and perhaps confuse the ELL. The guiding principle should be to avoid extremes when it comes to grammar and to assess the student and the situation, to offer grammar instruction when beneficial, and to avoid grammar instruction if such explanations will be too complicated. For example, explaining the definite article system in English can be complicated especially for ESL students whose L1 lacks an article system. However, short explanations in a meaningful context can help students through time.

❺ **Misconception:** Listening and reading are the easiest skills to acquire in a second language.
Truth: All four language skills (speaking, listening, reading, and writing) present unique learning challenges.

Traditionally textbook publishers and L2 teachers have noted a divide in second language skills between active skills (speaking and writing) and passive skills (listening and reading). Supposedly, the former are more difficult. An April 2005 *Washington Post* article discussed students choosing to study Latin instead of modern languages.

☼ Media Spotlight

Students generally memorize verb endings and adjective and noun declensions, translate classic Roman literature, and learn about Roman history. Some students who have trouble learning to speak modern languages—the hardest element of language learning—sometimes take Latin instead (Straus, 2005).

When communicating in a second language, there is little if anything that resembles passivity. In learning a second language, listening is not a passive skill; it does not just happen like in a first language. We have to work at it, and try as we might, we still occasionally miss things. Communicating via the telephone is even worse. There are no visual cues, and so listening to the speaker is even more difficult. Reading, as reading specialists (Ediger, 2001) will attest, is a very engaging activity and even more so in a second language.

Many ELL have fairly advanced speaking skills. They can circumlocute (use other words to convey a message when the speaker does not know the exact word) and make themselves understood. However, it is a false assumption that this speaking ability indicates that listening comprehension will be even more advanced since it is passive. An ELL can have trouble following classroom instruction even though he or she has advanced speaking skills. Research by Christison and Krahnke (1986) indicates that students value "the importance in academic work of the receptive skills of reading and listening over the productive skills of speaking and writing" (p. 61). This runs counter to intuition that would have us teach speaking and writing over listening and reading. Once teachers realize that receptive skills are not acquired as easily, they can incorporate the teaching of these skills into their pedagogy.

Implications for Teachers

In second language instruction, we should give equal instructional time to all aspects of the new language. Teachers with ELLs need to develop the habit of repeating key vocabulary and explaining terms that may not be familiar to the students, and should not assume that students have the aural skills necessary to follow classroom instruction. Listening and reading skills are not easy and cannot be overlooked in lesson planning. Mainstream teachers must do this as well.

Activities for Teachers

Activity 1: Graduation Requirements

Using the Internet, search for high school graduation requirements in different states. Check college graduation requirements around the country for the same information. Do most require study of a foreign language? What level of proficiency is required, and how is the students' proficiency gauged?

Activity 2: ESL Curriculum

Compose a letter to the U.S. Secretary of Education proposing a comprehensive plan for language instruction for ESL students. What are the best methods? How should school districts allocate resources?

Activity 3: Court Cases

- *Lau vs. Nichols* (1974) Summary: The Supreme Court ruled that a group of Chinese-speaking students had been denied access to education due to language barriers. The court ruled unanimously that schools are responsible for assisting students with basic English skills.

- *Plyer vs. Doe* (1982) Summary: The Supreme Court ruled that schools cannot deny access to education to undocumented immigrant children.

- *Pena vs. Board of Education City of Atlanta* (1985): Summary: A federal court ruled that school districts could not charge tuition to the parents of immigrant students.

The U.S. Supreme Court recognized that helping immigrants learn English improves society. In *Lau vs. Nichols* and *Plyer vs. Doe,* the Court ruled that denying immigrants access to education based on language or immigrant status is unconstitutional and ultimately harmful to society. Read the original opinions, and see if you agree with the Court's decisions and its reasoning.

Additional Resources

- The Center for Applied Linguistics *(www.cal.org)* is a government-sponsored agency that provides many resources to those who teach a second language or have questions about learning a second language.
- The Educational Resource Information Center (ERIC) *(www.eric.ed.gov)* provides access to many research articles concerning second language learning.
- Former U.S. Senator Paul Simon contended that Americans and American institutions acquiesce to the belief that some people just cannot learn a second language. He wrote a thought-provoking book in 1988 entitled *The Tongue-Tied American: Confronting the Foreign Language Crisis* (published by Crossroads Publishing). Although written twenty years ago, the main premise of the book is still true: Americans are perfectly willing to praise the notion of bilingualism but are unwilling to take real steps to ensure a bilingual populace in this country. Simon cites some compelling reasons for wanting a bilingual populace: trade, national security, and cultural understanding.
- Stephen Krashen's 1996 book *Under Attack: The Case against Bilingual Education* (published by Language Education Associates) is an interesting treatment of the question of whether bilingual education works.
- Richard Rodriguez's book *Hunger of Memory* (published by Bantam, 1982) is an interesting exploration of bilingual education. In this controversial text, Rodriguez presents his experiences with learning English and why he opposes bilingual education.
- Nora Mota-Altman's (2003) essay "Con Respeto, I Am Not Richard Rodriguez" offers a rebuttal to Rodriguez's critique of bilingual education. Available at *www.writingproject.org*.

CHAPTER 4

Myths about Language and Society

> *Ever'body says words different ... Arkansas folks say'em differ-*
> *ent, and Oklahomy folks say'em different. And we seen a lady*
> *from Massachusetts, an' she said'em differentests of all. Couldn'*
> *hardly make out what she was sayin'.*
>
> —John Steinbeck, 1939

Language and society are linked; neither can exist without the other. We identify ourselves and others as members of language and dialect groups, as the character from John Steinbeck's *The Grapes of Wrath* points out. This has sociological and pedagogical ramifications. The study of this intersection of language and society is known as sociolinguistics, a very relevant and important area of language study for teachers of ELLs. Linguistic misconceptions are never more prevalent than when it comes to how people view language and dialects within a social context, and this chapter will examine some of the most pervasive sociolinguistic misconceptions and how they impact classrooms with ELLs. The misconceptions discussed in this chapter are:

1. Some people do not speak in a dialect.

2. Declaring English as the official language will unify the country.

3. Television, movies, and the Internet are aiding in the disappearance of dialects.

> **❶ Misconception**: Some people do not speak in a dialect.
> **Truth**: Everyone has a dialect.

Some people believe they have no dialect. It is everyone else that has one. An inherent part of becoming socialized in language is to make distinctions. Most people do not even realize that they are making distinctions; they are simply following an age-old pattern: My way of speaking is the *normal* way; their way of speaking is *different*. Ironically, the very thing that allows people to proudly identify with groups also allows them to discriminate against those that do not "belong."

This standard linguistic mantra that everyone has a dialect is not believed by all. In a linguistics class I was teaching at a university in the South, a student from Michigan adamantly opposed any assertion that she had a dialect. People from Michigan (her home state), she claimed, had no dialect. I tried to explain that the Michigan dialect, although very close to standard, is still a dialect, but she would not believe me. As a pre-service teacher, this student held an erroneous view of language that could influence her approach to language education and her expectations and policies in the classroom. For example, some teachers may assign a lower grade to a student's oral presentation if the teacher thought the student was maintaining a non-standard dialect. Again, the reality is that we all have dialects.

In any language, there will be an acknowledged standard dialect. This standard is chosen arbitrarily and the process by which one dialect is selected as standard by society is done in a largely unconscious manner. Samuel Johnson posited that looking at other social classes for language standards was irrational. He said that there is "an illogical reverence for social betters" (Aitchison, 1991). This *illogical reverence* explains some of the mysterious social forces that help determine a standard dialect. Choosing a standard dialect has more to do with sociology than linguistics.

In 1962 linguist William Labov conducted a study in which he observed a dialect shift on Martha's Vineyard in Massachusetts. He observed residents changing the pronunciation of the vowel in words like *right* and *wife* during the height of tourist season. The residents changed the vowel sounds closer to a sixteenth- or seventeenth-century pronunciation. They did so as an identity marker. When the tourists left, however, the residents changed their vowels back to where they had been before. All this was unconsciously done by the residents.

This demonstrates two things. First, it shows residents wanted to distinguish themselves from the tourists and did so by altering their dialect. Labov discovered that the vowel shift became more prominent when residents were trying to emphasize their status as local residents rather than tourists who flood into the area every summer. Second, it demonstrates that a standard dialect is linked to the speech community, and it may change, thus we have potentially as many different dialects of a language as we do speakers of that language because everyone has an accent.

Implications for Teachers

Teachers need to be aware that they themselves as well as their students manifest some non-standard dialect features in their speech. They also need to be able to point out these variations to their ELL students so they may better navigate the labyrinth of American dialects.

---

❷ **Misconception**: Declaring English as the official language will unify the country.
Truth: A multilingual society is not a fragmented society.

There is an interesting contradiction in attitudes toward bilingualism in the United States. On the one hand, there is the perception that linguistic homogeneity would bring social unity. "In my school, we have an English-only policy. If a student is speaking Spanish, he or she will be asked to stop. It's school policy. This is America and not a foreign country," according to one teacher in a linguistics class. On the other hand, people often forget how linguistically diverse the United States is and always has been. Perhaps that is why we do not have an official language in the United States, a fact that often surprises people. Although the founders considered declaring English the official language in 1789, they decided against it (Baron, 2005). A myth persists that declaring English as the official language will unify an increasingly fragmented country. A powerful lobby group known as U.S. English is behind much of the legislative pressure to declare English as the official language, which it believes will unify the country. Would declaring English the official language have the desired unifying effects? Teddy Roosevelt thought so. Those who support such a measure like to quote Roosevelt, who said:

> We have room for but one flag, the American flag, and this excludes the red flag, which symbolizes all wars against liberty and civilization, just as much as it excludes any foreign flag of a nation to which we are hostile.... We have room for but one language here, and that is the English language ... and we have room for but one sole loyalty and that is a loyalty to the American people. (1907)

Roosevelt wrote this in 1907 during one of the many great waves of immigration to the United States. Roosevelt was always a staunch promoter of assimilation for immigrants, both in language and culture. He echoed many in the United States who favored immigration, but only if there were also linguistic and cultural assimilation. One hundred years later, we are still having the same debate about language, culture, and immigration.

Those who agree with Roosevelt fear that a polyglot nation would fragment while a monolingual nation would unify, forgetting that the United States has always been a polyglot nation. Even Benjamin Franklin worried about linguistic fragmentation, but his quarrel was with German. As Franklin said,

> Why should Pennsylvania, founded by the English, become a Colony of Aliens, who will shortly be so numerous as to Germanize us instead of our Anglifying them, and will never adopt our Language or Customs, any more than they can acquire our Complexion?
>
> (Quoted 1751, in Baron, 2005)

Franklin's words reflect his concern that the Germans were too distinct in language and culture from the English to be able to assimilate. As Baron (2005) notes, Franklin was writing at a time when "the Germans were accused … of laziness, illiteracy, clannishness, a reluctance to assimilate, excessive fertility, and Catholicism" (¶ 14). He was also writing at a time when many school were educating their students in a language other than English. Schools in several parts of the country during Franklin's and in Roosevelt's time were educating students in a language other than English but, like today, this caused a great deal of anxiety. And as with the current debate on immigration, language was at the center of immigration, but clearly there were and are other issues at work, namely fear of the "other."

Franklin's concern with German immigrants and the German language reflects our current national debate about Latinos and Spanish. In 2006, some people protested that the words of the *Star-Spangled Banner* were translated into Spanish. This, they believed, was the beginning of the end of English and subsequently, our national unity. As one columnist said,

---

☼ Media Spotlight

People are bewildered, confused and some downright angry over the National Anthem being sung in Spanish. What is this "in your face," "we don't care," "get used to us" protest about anyway? Why did you come here in the first place, to stuff your nationality in our faces and change the country to something that won't be what you came here for in the first place? Don't you see that you are destroying the thing you want most from America? We never had to sing it in French, Italian, Vietnamese, African, German, Irish, Greek, Scandinavian, Portuguese, Canadian, Russian, Chinese, Japanese, Icelandic, or even for God's sake, Arabic! (Bechtol, *Gulf Breeze News,* 2007)

The emotions behind these strong words run deep. There is a feeling that a translation of the national anthem is almost sacrilegious, or at least this is a slap in the face to America. Of course, this editorial is about more than just language or a translation. The author is commenting on immigration in general and assimilation into the culture. Some groups, intimates the author, are better at assimilating, and he is using language as an example of this assimilation. In the current immigration debate, language and culture are two related issues that stir passions and make the debate on this issue all the more contentious.

The U.S. Hispanic community, among other communities, is often suspicious of "official English" movements that purport to be a linguistic unifying solution. They suspect ulterior motives that have nothing to do with unity, but with discrimination. Some Hispanic leaders assert that it has more to do with racial intolerance than a quest for linguistic homogeneity. *Newsweek* ran a story on this debate in 1989; the article raised the same issues, unity vs. discrimination, that we are facing today almost twenty years later. Frederick Erickson, a linguist, said in the 1989 article that, "[English-only movements] are a real cover for bigotry" (Salholz, Gonzalez, & Hurt, 1989, p. 22).

In August 2006, Hazleton, Pennsylvania, passed a city ordinance to declare English the official language for its business. This by itself does not seem too incendiary. However, the language ordinance was packaged with other city ordinances, including fining landlords for renting to illegal immigrants and suspending the business license of an employer who hires illegal immigrants. Opponents of this bill called the inclusion of the language ordinance "mean-spirited."

Attacking language is much safer than attacking specific groups. To do so does not typically bring condemnations and accusations of racism, but neither will pushing for English only solve the immigration debate. Banning languages or promoting one over another just does not help.

U.S. English makes some interesting points about unity and the effects of a single national language. The group notes that one national language can bind people together. The group's website is full of thought-provoking quotes from thinkers and politicians. Even Alexis Tocqueville, an eighteenth-century French observer of the American political systems, noted a language's unifying power in 1835 in *Democracy in America*: "The tie of language is perhaps the strongest and the most durable that can unite mankind" (p. 28).

As a linguist, I do not agree with U.S. English in its attempt to legislate English. Language takes care of itself. Legislating language policy when the language is so well established (as is English) has little effect but to inflame political sensitivities. Language and immigration issues seem to cause much anxiety, but language anxiety by the public is unwarranted. Worry instead about sound educational policies for ELLs.

This is not to say that language is never used as leverage in discriminatory practices, but when you try to legislate language, the only means to enforce it is through enforcement of non-discrimination legislation. The issue is not protecting language, but people. Housing, employment, and social services should not be denied to someone because he or she speaks another language or uses a non-standard dialect. However, it is difficult to prove that someone's language skills are not an impediment to certain jobs. The courts are very hesitant when it comes to ruling on discrimination when an employer claims English (or a certain variety of English) is essential to a specific job. In 1991 James Kahakua was denied advancement in his career as a meteorologist in Hawaii because his employer thought his Hawaiian Creole English would be unacceptable to many television viewers. Kahakua sued but lost his case because the courts agreed that a certain variety of language could be essential to the job (Lippi-Green, 1997).

Many immigrants to the United States are bilingual due to circumstances. The children of the immigrants grow up exposed to the home language and English outside the home. Children not born in the United States arrive with one language and then must learn a new language. As a result, they usually become bilingual. Few people doubt the advantage of being proficient in English in the United States, but the real question revolves around the question of legislating English.

The United States in not alone in trying to declare an official language. A Belgian town made news in 2006 ("Belgian Town Bans School French") for banning French from being spoken in its schools by students. The hope was to increase French-speaking students' acquisition of Dutch. Multilingual societies struggle with this issue, but sensible policies are possible if policymakers and teachers avoid overly strict and oppressive English-only policies.

Implications for Teachers

This misconception that one language will unify the country is not only wrong, but it can be detrimental to the English development of ELLs. If ELLs feel that their language is not wanted in the United States (and that is the impression given by aggressive lobbying for declaring English as official), then they are often less inclined to learn English or at least feel as though it is an imposition. Teachers of ELLs need to help educate colleagues and policymakers by pointing out that the United States has multilingual roots, and this does not deter English acquisition, but can in fact support it.

---

❸ **Misconception:** Television, movies, and the Internet are aiding in the disappearance of dialects.
Truth: The number of dialects of English is growing in the United States.

Most people would say that there are fewer dialects of English today than there were before the invention of TV, commercial aviation, and the Internet (Chambers, 1999). These technological advances are, they would argue, making all dialects disappear. It *seems* logical. We are all exposed to more standard English in the media, and many people travel more, so dialects could be disappearing. However, research indicates just the opposite. Research by Fought (2005), Chambers (1999), and Wolfram & Schilling-Estes (2006) has documented that dialects are not disappearing; rather, they are growing and expanding, and the modern media has little influence on dialects. Modern media can reflect dialects and spread lexical items that originate in one specific dialect (think here of *bling* or *cool*), but it does not diminish dialects. Dialects are actually more distinctive today than they have been in 100 years.

In a 2005 *Washington Post* article titled "Bay's Dialects Slowly Dying," the author states that "like many of the other dialects, St. George-ese is fading. Many of the watermen who spoke it have left, and in their place are newcomers from the Washington suburbs and elsewhere" (Fahrenthold, 2005, p. A1). There is no question that some localized dialects such as those on island communities on the East Coast are fading due to migrations and proximity to growing urban centers (Wolfram & Schilling-Estes, 2006), but regional ones such as general southern dialect are growing in the number of speakers due to migration patterns (Tillery & Bailey, 2005). We may be in the midst of a great shift (perhaps due to migration), but dialects will continue to develop and as Wolfram & Schilling-Estes (2006) note, "Dialects mark the regional and cultural cartography of America as much as any cultural artifact, and there is no reason to expect that they will surrender their emblematic role in American life in the future." So despite the seemingly singular uniformity encouraged by television, movies, and the Internet, dialects are not being annihilated.

Implications for Teachers

Dialects are here to stay. Teachers must familiarize themselves with dialect differences so they can help ELL students as they master not only academic and standard English, but also as they master features of local and regional dialects.

Activities for Teachers

Activity 1: Factors Influencing Dialects

One of the best ways to understand dialects and the ways that geography, age, gender, and race are crucial factors in their development, is to do a survey. The first step is to identify specific features of dialects. For example, how acceptable is the word *like* in conversational speech, as in *He's like, I don't think so.* Using a five-point scale to survey people from all walks of life would allow investigating how acceptance of this feature breaks down along geographic, age, gender, and racial lines. Another favorite feature that linguists have looked at is the name for a carbonated sweet drink: *soda, Coke, pop, soft drink*. Putting the results in a graph allows a visual representation of the results. By participating in such an exercise, we can gain a better understanding about regional dialects and how they function in society.

Activity 2: Analyzing Dialects

Videotape a class. Note the differences in the speech of the class. Ask students to analyze the differences. Such an activity may prove enlightening to teachers about their own unconscious teaching habits and help them to become even better teachers.

If you are an in-service teacher, videotape a class that you teach. Note the differences of the speech of the class. Ask students to analyze the differences. What are the distinctive features? Such an activity may prove enlightening to teachers and students about their own attitudes toward dialects in the classroom.

If you are not teaching, the next time you are at a meeting, listen closely to participants. If someone has a dialect that is non-standard for the area you live in or that differs from the national standard, try to list features that distinguish this dialect. Is it his/her grammar, word choice, or pronunciation that is the most noticeable?

Activity 3: Changes in Prestige

List some world events that affect a language's or a dialect's position of prestige.

Additional Resources

- *American Tongues* (Center for New American Media, 1987) is perhaps one of the best-known videos concerning dialects and attitudes toward them. It is essential viewing for any teacher who works with language or dialect minority students.

- The PBS series *Do You Speak American?* (2005) addresses many of the current language issues in the United States. The book, written by video narrators, is also worthy.

- The websites *www.americanrhetoric.com* and *www.millercenter. virginia.edu* offer many speeches for analysis. You can examine and analyze speeches and accents from different regions of the United States.

CHAPTER **5**

Myths about Language and Thinking

Language is the dress of thoughts.

—Samuel Johnson, 1779

At some point in a linguistics course, students question the relationship between language and thought. It occurs to students that somehow language and thought are connected, but they are not quite sure how. The lexicographer Samuel Johnson understood the relationship, but he did not know exactly how the two were related. For centuries people have pondered and questioned the connection between language and thought and have tried to answer one question: How does language influence thinking? In this final chapter, this question along with two misconceptions about language and cognition, are discussed:

1. Language determines how we think.
2. Politics, popular culture, and technology are corrupting English by limiting many traditional forms of English.

> ❶ **Misconception**: Language determines how we think.
> **Truth**: Language influences thought, but it does not determine it.

There is an idea that holds that thinking is restricted by a person's native language (or languages). Language's influence on thinking is addressed by the Sapir-Whorf Hypothesis that, while influential in linguistics and ESL research, should not be accepted without being qualified because it could lead to the myth that thinking is determined by language. The hypothesis, developed by linguist Benjamin Whorf (1897–1941) and his mentor Edward Sapir (1884–1939), stipulates that our thinking is *determined* and even *limited* by the language we speak. This hypothesis is also known as linguistic determinism because language determines our thinking and our perception of reality. Whorf was not a professional linguist but rather a fire prevention expert who worked for Hartford Fire Insurance. It was his work with Hartford that led him to many business trips to the southwest region of the United States where he gained a special interest in Native American languages, which ultimately resulted in his theory of linguistic determinism.

Whorf developed this theory during his work with Native American languages, particularly Hopi. His work with these languages led him to the belief that speakers of different languages view the world differently. Whorf was convinced that since Hopi and English are so different structurally, semantically, and lexically, speakers of these languages must think differently and, consequently, view the world differently. For example, he noted that English has a grammatical affix (the suffix -*ed*) to express past tense, while in Hopi, no such tense markers exist. Whorf claimed that the lack of tense markers caused Hopi speakers to conceptualize time differently, not as linear passage of events like English speakers.

In 1940, Whorf published an article in M.I.T.'s *Technology Review* titled "Science and Linguistics" (reprinted in Carroll, 1956). In this article, Whorf argued against what he claimed was the traditionally held belief that languages do not contribute to the development of thoughts; the prevailing wisdom (according to Whorf) was that all the world's languages simply communicate ideas. He argued different languages do more than simply communicate thoughts; individual languages, he insisted, are the "shaper of thoughts" and thus different languages will cause speakers of those languages to generate different sorts of thoughts. Speakers of English will have different thoughts than speakers of French or any other language. His famous quote expands on this idea that thoughts are shaped by language:

> We dissect nature along lines laid down by our native languages. The categories and types that we isolate from the world of phenomena we do not find there because they stare every observer in the face; on the contrary, the world is presented in a kaleidoscopic flux of impressions which has to be organized by our minds—and this means largely by the linguistic systems in our minds. We cut nature up, organize it into concepts, and ascribe significances as we do, largely because we are parties to an agreement that holds throughout our speech community and is codified in the patterns of our language. The agreement is, of course, an implicit and unstated one, but its terms are absolutely obligatory; we cannot talk at all except by subscribing to the organization and classification of data which the agreement decrees. (Carroll, 1956)

Note that Whorf used the word *obligatory* when describing one's perception of reality and language. The language determines and obligates us to think in a certain way.

This idea of language determining our perception of reality has interesting social and pedagogical implications; it has been used to justify oppressive language policies such as British colonial policies in India that sought to replace Indian languages in schools with English. In 1835, Thomas Macaulay, a member of the Supreme Council of India, wrote a famous document in which he proclaimed that English must replace the language of the "Hindoos" [sic] in the Indian education system because English, with its rich vocabulary, will allow natives of India to think better, particularly when it comes to scientific and other non-fiction subjects. Language for Macaulay (like Whorf) determined thinking and scientific perceptual abilities. I do not imply that Whorf developed his ideas with any intent to suppress other languages, but rather this idea (which preceded his scientific formulation) gave rise to oppressive language policies. This kind of thinking was behind the attempt to "eradicate all the Native American languages, particularly those of the Plains tribes." As N. G. Taylor, president of the Commission on Indian Affairs, said in 1868:

> through sameness of language is produced sameness of sentiment, and thoughts; customs and habits are molded and assimilated in the same way, and thus in the process of time the differences producing trouble would have gradually obliterated. (Quoted in Lippi-Green, 1997, p. 115)

Taylor and his commission convinced others that if all the Native Americans spoke English, then their thinking would be more like that of the white Americans, and this would help assimilation. The idea was that they would then think like "Americans" because they had the same language. Of course, we understand today that even if they had learned English, there would still have been many cultural differences completely unrelated to sameness of language.

In the novel *1984* George Orwell (1983) described a government that controlled the population and its thinking through control of language. With "Newspeak" (the government's language), the bureaucracy mandated a strict control on language that they said would shape and limit thinking and create a government-controlled perception of reality.

These examples illustrate a common misconception that language determines thinking. This idea, formalized in the Sapir-Whorf Hypothesis, is a common and misleading notion because it implies that thinking or even ideas cannot exist without language. But they can. The English language contains examples of sexist language. For example, the many occupations that end in –*man*: *fireman, policeman,* and *chairman.* But these occupations are obviously not limited to men. These terms, though gender specific, can completely limit people's perception of who can do these jobs. Perhaps they might influence society's thinking about these jobs, but these words do not completely restrict thinking so extremely that women could not consider them, at least not in the twenty-first century. The Whorfian hypothesis, if taken to the extreme, is untenable for that very reason: Concepts exist even without words.

Linguists today claim that thinking may be *influenced* by a language (a weak version of the theory), but it is not *determined* by language (the strong version of the theory). If the Sapir-Whorf Hypothesis is true in its strong form, then translation would be impossible. Certain ideas or concepts would be so inherently linked to a particular language that ever translating them would be impossible, but this is not the case. While it is true that some ideas are more difficult to translate than others, bilinguals would agree that one way or another, we can translate even the most culturally bound concepts. The idea transcends language.

While the Sapir-Whorf Hypothesis has fallen into disfavor among linguists, experienced ESL researchers and teachers would be quick to point out that at least in its weak form, the theory has validity. Robert Kaplan presented the idea of contrastive rhetoric (a theory in composition research that stipulates that writers from different cultural and linguistic backgrounds construct written arguments differently). He published a seminal article titled "Cultural Thought Patterns in Inter-Cultural Education" in 1966 that deals with this issue. In his article, Kaplan compares the structure of written arguments in English with Semitic languages, Romance languages, Oriental [sic] languages, and Russian. He concludes that, due to cultural and linguistic differences, written arguments are structured differently in the different languages. The structures differ in directness, format, and a host of other ways, and he attributes this in part to linguistic traits of the languages. What makes this a weak form of the Whorfian hypothesis is that Kaplan does not imply that the structures are obligatory, just that the languages influence the structural differences.

Despite methodological problems, this article and its conclusions continue to influence ESL writing teachers. The most obvious pedagogical implication of Kaplan's idea relates to writing tasks. To write in a second language necessitates being able to think and compose written texts in that language and to write the essay in a coherent fashion. Students must be able to produce cogent arguments in their academic papers. However, some ESL writers have difficulty with this, and it does not always stem from grammatical and lexical errors but from using a different set of rules when it comes to argumentation. Kaplan says that written rhetorical strategies are not universal but vary and are linked to culture and language. So an ESL student may construct a different kind of argument for his or her English class because his native language and culture dictate a certain style of argumentation that may run counter to what is expected in American classrooms.

What teachers may not be aware of is that this is often due to different approaches to rhetoric stemming from linguistic and cultural differences. At the risk of overgeneralizing, let me offer this example: Chinese ESL students will construct written arguments that are far different from those of their Latin American classmates. The Chinese students' papers tend to be less direct and less forceful than that of the Latin American students. Chinese students use more qualifiers and more appeal to authority, while Latin American students place more emphasis on developing a relationship with the reader.

The case of Indian writers of English offers further evidence that different rhetorical strategies are influenced by language. Even though English is used as a primary language of instruction for many Indians and the students of India who attend American universities are quite fluent in English, their essays lack the directness that is so highly prized in American universities. Such direct methods of argumentation are discouraged in Indian schools. A long and thorough introduction about the subject before addressing it is much more valued in the Indian system. As an interesting sidenote, many scholars argue that English in India is being altered to fit the cultural and cognitive realities in India (Kachru, 1992) so that "Indian English" will change shape to fit the needs of India.

It would be difficult to determine how much of this is due to linguistic differences and how much is due to cultural differences, but the end result is the same: ESL compositions will have a different feel to them and may not look like American compositions. Certainly ELLs need to learn the conventions of standard writing for an American academic setting. On the other hand, sometimes American educational institutions need to be more cosmopolitan in their judgment of what is acceptable writing.

Implications for Teachers

Contrastive rhetoric considerations have a place when teaching and evaluating ESL writing. Teachers of ESL students need to be aware of the influence of native languages on writing, both grammatically and rhetorically. This is not to suggest that teachers should not teach what American schools expect with their writing; however, it does make sense to consider that sometimes what seems fuzzy or not clearly organized to the American reader might not be the result of bad or sloppy writing. It could be the result of language and culture influencing, though not determining, thoughts and their expression in academic writing.

> ❷ **Misconception**: Politics, popular culture, and technology
> are corrupting English by limiting many traditional forms of
> English.
> **Truth**: English's traditional and innovative forms are
> flourishing.

Claims exist that the politically correct movement, popular culture, and modern technology are all corrupting English. But English users, despite modernity, are using traditional forms and innovative forms, and English is not being so trimmed down so as to limit students' thinking.

PC Language

Diane Ravitch published *The Language Police: How Pressure Groups Restrict What Students Learn* in 2004 in which she argued that attempts to police words in classrooms and in textbooks have dramatically affected school curricula. Ravitch takes to task the whole politically correct (PC) language movement (using language that does not offend groups) because she claims students are being done a disservice when political forces control language in an attempt to avoid offending and to eradicate biased thinking. In one of the book's appendixes, Ravitch offers a list of words and phrases that are restricted in the textbook publishing industry because they offend racial, gender, or class sensitivities. She offers examples of the extreme nature of the politically correct movement. Her appendix notes why certain words are banned. Some banned words are sexist because they privilege men (e.g., *airman, baseman, manly, man-of war,* and *unmanned*) or demean women (e.g., *busybody, coed, gal, maid, seamstress,* and *stewardess*). Some are racist (e.g., *colored, gringo, mulatto, oriental, savage,* and *swarthy*). Some disparage the disabled (e.g., *able-bodied, confined to a wheel chair, dumb, gimp, little person,* and *sickly*). She also lists images that are often censored, such as women sewing, Native Americans as warlike, and Irish policemen. Her point is not that some of these words are not offensive, but rather her point is that our language and our schools have become too obsessed with politically correct language.

Critics of the PC movement contend that when schools restrict teachers from using certain words that have been traditionally used or when these words are stigmatized in society, our language suffers and that perfectly good words are being eliminated from our collective lexicon. They think that this hyper-sensitivity will diminish our freedom of speech and impoverish English by eliminating what once were viable and sophisticated lexical choices, which will eliminate our ability to cogently express thoughts.

One example is the word *refugee* to describe the victims of Hurricane Katrina. The dictionary definition of *refugee* is a "person displaced by war or natural disaster." But some residents of New Orleans objected to the word *refugee*. Critics such as Jesse Jackson and members of the Congressional Black Caucus have claimed that if the displaced residents had not been African Americans, then *refugee* would not have been the word choice of the media and the government (Pierre & Farhi, 2005, p. C1). The website *Language Monitor* lists some of the more interesting examples of a PC language–inspired lexicon: *deferred success* for *failure* and *thought shower* for *brainstorm* (to avoid insensitivity to epileptics).

From a linguistic standpoint, the movement has made us aware that words and language have a unique and powerful force and that we have to be aware of how we use them. In this sense, the PC movement can be positive. For example, we no longer use *Mongoloidism* to describe someone with Down's Syndrome. We do not inflict those who are disabled with negative labels, such as *retarded* or *deaf-mute*. These are good things.

The PC movement came about precisely to protect groups who have traditionally been demeaned by language: the disabled, women, and minorities. Work by Deborah Tannen (1990) and Robin Lakoff (1975) introduced the ways that gender plays a large role in communicative styles. The PC movement took this a step further and demonstrated how women are often excluded in communication by the words used in professional settings (e.g., *chairman, firemen,* the so-called generic *he*). Work by John Baugh (2000) discusses how minority groups too have been excluded or even victimized by language that is offensive. The PC movement seeks to correct this by seeking to control language. Ravitch's book notes that there can be extremes in education policies when the PC movement is implemented. However, from a linguistic standpoint, language is not so fragile and so limited that a movement such as the PC movement can really have long-lasting effects on the language. Perhaps such movements raise consciousness, but they will not control how we think because language is creative and, ultimately, it will create new words once old ones fall into disfavor or to fill a perceived need.

This issue of PC language has an added dimension for the ESL classroom. Elizabeth Claire wrote a teacher resource book entitled *Dangerous English* in which she discusses examples of un-PC words that teachers should educate ESL students about. This is a good idea because ESL learners are likely to be unaware of how offensive seemingly innocuous words or phrases are and that they should be avoided. For their part, teachers need to understand and to be able to explain the implications of the PC movement. We should be able to explain it to ESL students who are faced with the challenge of not only learning English but also navigating the minefield of the PC language world.

Popular Culture

Most people would say swearing is in poor taste and that popular culture (TV, music, movies) is more laced with profanity than ever before. Some think that swearing simply shows a lack of social awareness, while others argue that it indicates a lack of morality and points to a potential further decline in society. Pavel Bispalenko, a Russian local government official, is leading a charge to curb swearing in Russia by placing posters over swear words on walls. As Bispalenko says, "Swearing is a moral disease, a social illness. Scientists have proved that people who use bad words turn into bad people, so the aim of our campaign is to improve the health and moral standing of our nation" (qtd. in McEnery, 2006). Note the use of science. McEnery uses this quote to illustrate the misconception that swearing produces "bad" people.

Tony McEnery, a linguist, takes exception to notions that swearing is increasing or shows a moral collapse. In his 2006 book *Swearing in English: Bad Language, Purity, and Power from 1586 to the Present,* he demonstrates that cursing has always been with us and always will be. He admits that it is extremely difficult to verify the number of swear words used in speech from a historical perspective, but he provides evidence that swearing is part of every language and that the amount of swearing has not necessarily risen. He suggests that swearing is often used as an easy target for social ills that have less to do with language and more to do with social choices and behavior (McEnery, 2006).

McEnery proposes a sociological hypothesis for swearing. He shows that with the rise of the middle class in England in the seventeenth and eighteenth centuries, there arose a more conscious awareness and stigmatization of swearing. In essence, he maintains the middle class used swearing as a dividing line between them and the working class (McEnery, 2006). This is not unlike the use of dialect and accent to differentiate social classes as noted in Chapter 1. McEnery supports his theory by showing the working class using swear words as a sign of solidarity.

Beyond these theoretical treatments of swearing, there is also the emotional impact of swearing. I think here too cursing acts as a divider that can distinguish the native and non-native speakers of a language. Cursing does not attack a group directly; so, in this sense, many swear words are acceptable depending on the context. McEnery's research suggests that swearing in English is no more prevalent today than it was hundreds of years ago. However, during what he calls "moral panics," people are much more aware of swearing in society and the popular media. Like the PC movement, though, this does not indicate a lack of facility with the English language by the young, just that we become more aware of swearing given what is happening in society.

Technology

Instant-messaging (IM) and text-messaging are sometimes considered contributors to students' lack of literacy skills these days. This is not the first time technology has been blamed for declining literacy rates or even declining language standards. Television, radio, and even the type-writer have been blamed for declining literacy and language standards. However, the lament seems especially intense now with new computer technology.

Again, these fears of literacy breakdown are unfounded. Early research (Lewis & Fabos, 2005) indicates that indeed this technology, while not enforcing standard spelling, does in fact promote literacy, albeit a differ-ent kind of literacy. Simply put, it could motivate students (ELLs and native-English speakers) to become more involved with texts. Many more longitudinal studies of the effects of technology on literacy or on the language itself are needed to resolve the issue.

Cliff Nass, a professor at Stanford University, is researching how future technologies will incorporate voice activation. Part of Nass's research centers on questions of whether this technology could be used to eliminate or at least ameliorate language stereotypes associated with certain dialects. In other words, if we use non-standard dialects as the voice interface with sophisticated machines, that has the potential to alter perceptions of that dialect. Computers can be programmed to understand or use any dialect, so a non-standard dialect could be used.

Technology, whether in IMing or through voice interface, will have implications for language use. Certainly computer games and email have developed a sort of informality, but this need not affect more traditional and formal modes of written and oral discourse. Children are capable of grasping how language is used differently in different settings. We all change registers of language depending on the situation. Technology in this sense can be a great tool to teach children this and the ways that language can be adapted to the situation. Technology will not ruin all formality in language and thinking. We must develop new ways of look-ing at literacy as technology continues to develop.

Implications for Teachers

Teachers should understand that every language has curse words and cursing is not a localized phenomenon. This can be a difficult aspect of the language to teach and, in fact, most language teachers avoid the topic. However, if teachers do not make students aware of these objectionable words, then students may unwittingly utilize them in ways that are extremely embarrassing and detrimental to their success. Each teacher must gauge the need and appropriateness for such discussions in each classroom.

Teachers of ELLs should not be too quick to dismiss technology as harmful to learning English. Text messaging and other computer functions may be interesting for ELLs, especially if their friends are using them. Technology has many useful applications to teaching, but of course ELLs need access to standard and academic English as well.

Activities for Teachers

Activity 1: PC Classrooms

The whole issue of political correctness has enormous implications for the classroom. Examine websites that deal with the banning of certain texts for the use of offensive words. Ask colleagues how their "language" has changed in the classroom in the last few years. Are there words that are "off-limits" that years ago were not. Ask practicing ESL teachers how they approach vulgarity/obscenity in the classroom. Is it important for ESL children to know these words?

Activity 2: Swearing in School

Look up school policies on swearing. Do districts have a state policy for students who swear? What are the consequences of swearing?

Activity 3: Technology

Do you believe that students are being influenced in their writing by their use of technology (such as instant messaging)? What evidence do you see of this?

Some teachers allow text messaging abbreviations in the classroom for certain assignments to get students excited about writing. Do you agree with this? Would there be too much pressure from the community and the administration to not do this?

Can ESL students benefit from using the abbreviations in text messaging as a way to increase their use of English?

Epilogue

Twenty years ago, searching for academic information was a time-consuming task. Libraries had card catalogues, big file cabinets with small cards that one had to explore to find a text on a subject. Finding articles in periodicals was even more laborious. Researching took time, and there was no guarantee of finding the right information in a particular library. Professors and students often had to visit other libraries to find the information they needed. All of that has changed with the Internet and electronic databases. Most of today's undergraduates have never even seen a card catalogue, and some undergraduates have never even been to the university's library because they can do most of their research on their computer. Finding information can now be done relatively easily, quickly, and remotely. Despite this (or maybe because an abundance of information is so accessible), there is much misinformation about many topics, including language learning. There is so much to access that it becomes difficult to distinguish fact from fiction, allowing misconceptions to take root. The media is just as susceptible to this misinformation as anyone, and the media can perpetuate myths by passing on misinformation to a broad audience.

In this text I have discussed the misconceptions that continue to grow about language and linguistics through the media, popular culture, and everyday interaction in spite of all the well-researched linguistic information available. In my teaching of linguistics for the past ten years, I have heard many of the same myths over and over in class and out of class. The misconceptions have taken root but, they can, I believe, be weeded out.

The "information age" makes exciting possibilities for research and dissemination of information. This information age will undoubtedly have ramifications on language and language policies as newer and more technology interfaces with language. The core truths about human language will remain stable because language is a culture entity as well as a communicative one. This reality and the undoing of linguistic misconceptions explored in this text are important to keep in mind as we seek to help ELLs learn English and have a positive learning experience in the process.

The linguistic misconceptions addressed in this book are a beginning to explore further language learning. The education of ELLs in mainstream and ESL classes is a reality of the American educational system that will not disappear anytime in the near future. Therefore, teachers will be critical players in meeting the language learning needs of their students. This role will include:

- being knowledgeable and able to distinguish myths from realities about language learning
- being vocal and effective advocates for the ELLs at classroom, school, district, and public venues
- being a well-informed resource for parents, policymakers, and colleagues

In short, linguistics matters because language affects us all. American society is profoundly affected by our attitudes about and understanding of language, and the English language learner is even more so as laws and policies continue to be made to address language struggles in the classroom and workplace.

REFERENCES

Aitchison, J. (1991). *Language change: Progress or decay.* Cambridge, UK: Cambridge University Press.

Andrews, D. (2002, May). Are toddlers tuning in too much? *Ladies Home Journal,* 141.

Atkins, C. (1993). Do employment recruiters discriminate on the basis of nonstandard dialects? *Journal of Employment Counseling, 30,* 108–119.

Baron, D. (1996, September 8). Lingua blanka—Let's be done with the poor old mother tongue. *The Washington Post,* C5.

———. (2005). The legendary English-only vote of 1795. Retrieved from the *Do You Speak American Website,* http://www.pbs.org/speak/

Barry, D. (1988). *Dave Barry's greatest hits.* New York: Ballantine Books.

Bauer, L., & Trudgill, P. (Eds.). (1999). *Language myths.* London: Penguin Books.

Baugh, J. (2000). *Beyond Ebonics: Linguistic pride and racial prejudice.* Oxford, UK: Oxford University Press.

Bechtol, T. (2007, February 7). I just can't get over it. *Gulf Breeze News,* 1B.

Belgian town bans school French. (2006). Retrieved from the BBC News Online website, http://news.bbc.co.uk

Bollag, B. (2007, June 8). MLA report calls for transformation of foreign-language education. *Chronicle of Higher Education, 53*(40), A12.

Bragg, M. (Producer). (2004). *Many tongues called English, one world language.* [Television broadcast.] Princeton, NJ: Films for Humanities.

Brown, H. D. (2007). *Principles of language learning and teaching.* White Plains, NY: Longman.

Brown, R. (1973). *A first language: The early stages.* Cambridge, MA: Harvard University Press.

Bryson, B. (2001). The *mother tongue: English and how it got that way.* New York: Harper Perennial.

Carroll, J. (Ed.). (1956). *Language, thought, and reality: Selected writings of Benjamin Lee Whorf.* Cambridge: Technology Press of Massachusetts Institute of Technology.

Cavanaugh, M. (1996). History of teaching English as a Second Language. *English Journal, 85,* 40–44.

Chambers, J. K. (1999). TV makes people sound the same. In L. Bauer & P. Trudgill (Eds.), *Language myths* (pp. 123–131). London: Penguin Books.

Chomsky, N. (1959). A review of B. F. Skinner's verbal behavior. *Language, 35,* 26–58.

————. (2004). Knowledge of language as a focus of inquiry. In B. Lust & C. Foley (Eds.), *First language acquisition: The essential readings* (pp. 15–24). Malden, MA: Blackwell Publishing.

Christison, M.A., & Krahnke, K. (1986). Student perceptions of academic language study. *TESOL Quarterly, 20*, 61–81.

Clair, E. (2000). *Dangerous English.* McHenry, IL: Delta Systems.

Clearfield, A. (2005, February 19). Religion, morality not the same. *The Eagle,* p. B5.

Close, R. (2004). *Television and language development in the early years: A review of the literature.* Commissioned by the National Literary Trust. London. Retrieved November 1, 2007, from http://www.literacytrust.org.uk/Research/TV.pdf

Coates, T. (2004, May 26–June 1). Ebonics! Weird names! $500 shoes! Shrill Bill Cosby and the speech that shocked black America. Retrieved from *The Village Voice* website, http://www.villagevoice.com

Collier, V., & Thomas, W. (1997). *School effectiveness for language minority students.* National Clearinghouse for Bilingual Education. Retrieved November 1, 2007, from http://www.ncela.gwu.edu/pubs/resource/effectiveness/thomas-collier97.pdf

Crystal, D. (2003). *English as a global language.* Cambridge, UK: Cambridge University Press.

————. (2007). *How language works: How babies babble, words change meaning, and languages live or die.* London: Penguin.

Cummins, J. (1996). *Negotiating identities: Education for empowerment in diverse societies.* Los Angeles: California Association for Bilingual Education.

————. (2000). *Language, power, and pedagogy. Bilingual children in the crossfire.* Clevedon, UK: Multilingual Matters.

Cunneff, T. (2002, July 15). Insider. *People Magazine,* 43.

Curtis, S. (1977). *Genie: A psycholinguistic study of a modern-day "wild child."* New York: Academic Press.

Dougherty, D. (2000, June). Baby talk. *Atlanta Parenting Magazine,* 56.

Eble, C. (1996). *Slang and sociability: In-group languages among college students.* Chapel Hill: University of North Carolina Press.

Echevarria, J., Vogt, M., & Short, D. (2004). Issues of reading development and special education for English learners. In J. Echevarria (Ed.), *Making content comprehensible for English learners: The SIOP model* (pp. 163–177). Boston: Allyn & Bacon.

Ediger, A. (2001). Teaching children literacy skills in a second language. In M. Celce-Murcia (Ed.), *Teaching English as a second or foreign language* (pp. 153–169). Boston: Heinle & Heinle.

Ellis, R. (1994). *The study of second language acquisition.* Oxford, UK: Oxford University Press.

Eskenazi, M. (2000, December 11). The new case for Latin. *Time,* 61.

Fahrenthold, D. (2005, February 19). Bay's dialects slowly dying. *The Washington Post,* A1.

Farkas, S. (2003). What immigrants say about life in the United State. Retrieved from the website, Public Agenda. http://www.migrationinformation.org

Folse, K. (2004). *Vocabulary myths: Applying second language research to classroom teaching.* Ann Arbor: University of Michigan Press.

Fought, C. (2005). Are dialects fading? Retrieved November 6, 2007, from http://www.pbs.org/speak/ahead/mediapower/dialect/index.html

Frank, R. (1993, February 17). Laissez-Faire bilingualism in California. *International Herald Tribune.* Retrieved from www.iht.com

Freeman, J. (1998, April 5). Teletubbies need no translation. *Boston Globe,* D5.

Frese, D. (2005). Divided by a common language: The Babel Proclamation and its influence in Iowa history. Retrieved from http://www.historycooperative.org/journals/ht/39.1/frese.html#FOOT27

Fromkin, V., Rodman, R., & Hyams, N. (2006). *An introduction to language* (8th ed.). Boston: Heinle & Heinle.

Gardner, R., & Lambert, W. (1972). *Attitudes and motivation in second language learning.* Rowley, MA: Newbury House.

Giles, H., & Niedzielski, N. (1999). Italian is beautiful, German is ugly. In L. Bauer & P. Trudgill (Eds.), *Language myths* (pp. 85–93). London: Penguin Books.

Gingrich, N. (2006, April 26). Honesty in immigration: We need a firm foundation of law. Retrieved from the *National Review Online* website, http://www.nationalreview.com

Graddol, D., Leith, D., & Swann, J. (1996). *English: History, diversity and change.* London: Routledge.

Holman, J. (1998, January). Learning a language—language learning among children. *Better Homes and Gardens,* 40–41.

Hornberger, N. (2002, April). *Ideology, ecology, and biliteracy: Implementing multilingual language policies in community and classroom.* Paper presented at the meeting of the American Association of Applied Linguistics Conference, Salt Lake City, UT.

Hyatt, P. (Producer). (2004, June 7). *Dr. Phil Show.* [Television broadcast.] Los Angeles: Peteski Productions.

Jensen, A. (1969). How much can we boost IQ and scholastic achievement? *Harvard Educational Review, 39,* 1–123.

Johnson, J., & Newport, E. (1989). Critical period effects in second language learning: The influence of maturational state on the acquisition of English as a Second Language. *Cognitive Psychology, 21,* 60–99.

Johnson, S. (2006). *Lives of the English poets: Waller, Milton, Cowley.* Charleston, SC: Bibliobazaar. (Originally published 1779.)

Kachru, B. (1992). *The other tongue: English across cultures.* Urbana: University of Illinois Press.

Kaplan, R. (1966). Cultural thought patterns in intercultural education. *Language Learning, 16,* 1–12.

Kelly, R. (1981). *The Andy Griffith show.* Winston-Salem, NC: John F. Blair.

Knapp, D. (1996). Jackson, Oakland school board discuss Ebonics. Retrieved from *CNN Interactive.* http://www.cnn.com/US/9612/30/ebonics/

Krashen, S. (1996). *Under attack: The case against bilingual education.* Burlingame, CA: Language Education Associates.

Krashen, S., & Terrel, T. (1983). *The natural approach: Language acquisition in the classroom.* Oxford, UK: Pergamon.

Kuhl, P. K. (2004). Early language acquisition: Cracking the speech code. *Nature Reviews Neuroscience, 5,* 831–843.

Labov, W. (1962). *The social history of a sound change on the island of Martha's Vineyard, Massachusetts.* Master's thesis, Columbia University.

———. (1972). *Sociolinguistic patterns.* Philadelphia: University of Pennsylvania Press.

Lakoff, R. (1975). *Language and woman's place.* New York: Harper & Row.

Lenneberg, E. (1964). The capacity for language acquisition. In J. Fodor & J. Katz (Eds.), *The structure of language: Readings in the philosophy of language* (pp. 579–603). Englewood Cliffs, NJ: Prentice Hall.

Lewis, C., & Fabos, B. (2005). Instant messaging, literacies, and social identities. *Reading Research Quarterly, 40,* 470–501.

Lightbown, P., & Spada, N. (1999). *How languages are learned.* Oxford, UK: Oxford University Press.

Lindholm-Leary, K. (2001). *Dual language education.* Clevedon, UK: Multilingual Matters.

Lippi-Green, R. (1997). *English with an accent: Language, ideology, and discrimination in the United States.* New York: Routledge.

Macaulay, T. (1835). Minutes of 2 February 1835 meeting on Indian education. Retrieved November 10, 2007, from http://shelterbelt.com/ARCHIVE/macaulayminutes.html

Mackey, W. (1978). The importance of bilingual education models. In J. E. Alatis (Ed.), *Georgetown University round table on language and linguistics: International dimensions of bilingual education* (pp. 1–18). Washington, DC: Georgetown University Press.

MacNeil, R., & Cran, W. (2005). *Do you speak American?* Orlando, FL: Harcourt.

McCrum, R., MacNeil, R., & Cran, W. (1986). *The story of English.* New York: Viking.

McDonald's not lovin' 'McJob' dictionary definition. Retrieved November 10, 2003, from http://www.cnn.com

McEnery, T. (2006). *Swearing in English: Bad language, purity, and power from 1586 to the present.* New York: Routledge.

McLaughlin, B. (1992). Myths and misconceptions about second language learning: What every teacher needs to unlearn. Retrieved from National Center on Cultural Diversity and Second Language Learning website, http://repositories. cdlib.org/crede/ncrcdslleducational/EPR05/

Marshall, B. (1996, February 27). Talk on the wild side: Old-style grammarians are under pressure to loosen their grip on the English language. *The Guardian*, 4.

Marshall, J. (2006, December 8). Teaching grammar could stop mod violence. *Times Educational Supplement.* Retrieved May 2007, from http://www.tes.co.uk

Modern Language Association. (2006). Foreign language instruction: Implementing the best teaching methods. *Research Points*, 4, 1.

Montessori, M. (1995). *The absorbent mind.* New York: Henry Holt and Company. (Originally published 1949).

Morning edition. (2006, May 31). [Radio broadcast.] National Public Radio.

Mota-Altman, N. (2003). Con respeto, I am not Richard Rodriguez. *English Language Learners Network.* Retrieved from the *National Writing Project* website, http:// www.writingproject.org

National Clearinghouse for English Language Acquisition. (2006). Retrieved May 10, 2007, from http://www.ncela.gwu.edu/stats/2_nation.htm

O'Connor, M. (2005, August 12). Salons sued over alleged language ban. *Chicago Tribune*, 9.

O'Grady, W., Archibald, J., Aronoff, M., & Rees-Miller, J. (2005). *Contemporary linguistics: An introduction.* Boston: Bedford/St. Martin's.

Orman, F. (1927, August 16). Observations on reform of the English language. *New York Times*, 16.

Orwell, G. (1983). *1984.* New York: New American Library.

Patkowski, M. (1980). The sensitive period for the acquisition of syntax in a second language. *Language Learning*, 30, 444–472.

Pierre, R., & Farhi, P. (2005, September 7). Refugee: A word of trouble. *The Washington Post*, C1.

Pinker, S. (1994). *The language instinct. How the mind creates language.* New York: William Morrow.

Piper, T. (1998). Chapter seven: Michael's miracle. In *Language and learning: The home and school years* (2nd ed.) (pp. 167–190). Des Moines, IA: Prentice Hall.

Pope, V. (1924, April 13). Poet laureate argues here for pure English. *New York Times.* Retrieved February 20, 2005, from the Proquest database.

Preston, D. (1999). They speak really bad English down south and in New York City. In L. Bauer & P. Trudgill (Eds.), *Language myths* (pp. 139–149). London: Penguin.

Public School Notes. (1923, June 6). *The New York Times,* 42.

Pullum, G., & Scholz, B. (2001). More than words. *Nature, 413,* 367.

Purnell, T., Idsardi, W., & Baugh, J. (1999). Perceptual and phonetic experiments on American English dialect identification. *Journal of Social Psychology, 18,* 10–30.

Ramirez, R. (2004). *We the people: Hispanics in the United States.* U.S. Census Bureau. http://www.census.gov/prod/2004pubs/census-18.pdf

Ravitch, D. (2003). *The language police: How pressure groups restrict what students learn.* New York: Vintage Books.

Redd, T., & Webb, K. (2005). *A teacher's introduction to African American English: What a writing teacher should know.* Urbana, IL: NCTE.

Reise, J. (Executive Producer). (2001, November 11). *NBC Nightly News.* [Television broadcast.] New York: National Broadcasting Company.

Rodriguez, R. (1982). *Hunger of memory: The education of Richard Rodriguez.* New York: Bantam Books.

Roduta, C. (2003, December 2). Latin being resurrected. *The News-Sentinel,* 1a.

Rutherford, W. (1987). *Second language grammar: Learning and teaching.* White Plains, NY: Addison-Wesley.

Safire, W. (1984). *I stand corrected: More on language.* New York: Times Books.

Salholz, E., Gonzalez, D., & Hurt, H. (1989, February 20). Say it in English. *Newsweek,* 22–23.

Schmidt, S. (2006, November 10). Babies need building blocks, not TV, research finds. *The Vancouver Sun,* A1.

Searchinger, G. (Producer). (1994). Human Language Series. [Television broadcast]. New York: Equinox Films.

Simon, P. (1988). *The tongue-tied American: Confronting the foreign language crisis.* New York: Crossroad Publishing Company.

Skinner, B. F. (1957). *Verbal behavior.* New York: Appleton-Century-Crofts.

Steele, S. (2006). *White guilt: How blacks and whites together destroyed the promise of the Civil Rights Era.* New York: HarperCollins.

Steinbeck, J. (2002). *The grapes of wrath*. New York: Penguin Books.

Straus, V. (2005, April 26). Latin: A language alive and well. *The Washington Post*.

Talk of the southern mountaineer. (1901, April 7). *New York Times*, 23.

Tannen, D. (1990). *You just don't understand: Women and men in conversation*. New York: HarperCollins.

Tillery, J., & Bailey, G. (2005). *Southern American*. Retrieved November 6, 2007, from http://www.pbs.org/speak/seatosea/americanvarieties/southern/sounds/#bailey

Tocqueville, A. (1990). *Democracy in America*. New York: Vintage Books. (Originally published 1835).

Trudgill, P. (1999). The meaning of words should not be allowed to change. In L. Bauer & P. Trudgill (Eds.), *Language myths* (pp. 1–8). London: Penguin Books.

Tse, L. (2001). *"Why don't they learn English?" Separating fact from fallacy in the U.S. language debate*. New York: Teachers College Press.

Valdes, G. (2001). *Learning and not learning English: Latino students in American schools*. New York: Teachers College Press.

Walton, B. (2007, January 10). Speak the language of youth: Parents want children to start learning foreign tongues early. *USA Today*, D8.

Whitman, W. (1982). Slang in America. In J. Kaplan (Ed.), *Whitman: Prose and poetry* (pp. 1165–1170). New York: Library Classics of the United States. (Originally published 1888).

Williams, W. (2000). Declining standards. Retrieved from http://www.gmu.edu/departments/economics/wew/articles/00/standards.html

Winslow, R. (1997, July 10). How language is stored in brain depends on age. *Wall Street Journal*, B1.

Wolfram, W. (1999). Black children are verbally deprived. In L. Bauer & P. Trudgill (Eds.), *Language myths* (pp. 103–112). London: Penguin.

Wolfram, W., & Schilling-Estes, N. (2006). Language evolution or dying traditions? The state of American dialects. In W. Wolfram & B. Ward (Eds.), *American Voices: How dialects differ from coast to coast* (pp. 1–6). Malden, MA: Blackwell.

Wolfram, W., Adger, C., & Christian, D. (1999). *Dialects in schools and communities*. Mahwah, NJ: Lawrence Erlbaum.

Yang, C. (2006). *The ultimate gift: How children of the world learn and unlearn the languages of the world*. New York: Scribner.

Index